BORDER TERR

An Owner's Comp

?Y

BORDER TERRIERS
An Owner's Companion

Frank and Jean Jackson

The Crowood Press

First published in 1997 by
The Crowood Press Ltd
Ramsbury, Marlborough
Wiltshire SN8 2HR

www.crowood.com

Paperback edition 2003

British Library Cataloguing-in-Publication Data
A catalogue record for this book is available from the British Library.

ISBN 1 86126 640 5

Line-drawings by Annette Findlay

Typeset by Phoenix Typesetting, Burley-in-Wharfedale, West Yorkshire.

Printed and bound in Great Britain by The Bath Press.

Contents

Introduction

After spending more than three decades in close association with the breed, as well as with those who fervently share our interest, and having previously gone through a period of ten or fifteen years during which our association was more distant but our keen support no less sure, what follows cannot hope to be an objective assessment of the breed. It is the product of a sustained enthusiasm which might, at times, verge on the obsessive. We have been far too long involved with Border Terriers to know everything about them, nor would we claim to be experts. Only if one accepts Stephen Jay Gould's succinct definition – for 'country', read 'breed' – 'experts are people who have been in a country for more than twenty years or less than two' do we fall into that category.

Our first contact with the breed took place on the Lakeland Fells when we were enjoying a day out with the Blencathra. That would be in the late 1940s, but it was not until the late 1950s that circumstances allowed us to add a Border Terrier to our household. Even then there was no thought of becoming involved in the show scene: our interest was in sport and companionship. At the time, however, we were showing a Dalmatian and so it was almost inevitable that our Border Terrier would also be taken to shows; and when her success eclipsed anything we had been able to achieve with Dalmatians, the die was cast. She was not a top quality Border because her eyes were light and her muzzle rather too beak-like, but that does not detract from the value we attach to her first win – Sam's Cup for Best Special Beginner – nor from the show critique in which she is described by one of the world's top judges as having 'a keen dark eye and a short strong muzzle'.

Our first litter produced a CC winner, a bitch which, had we had the knowledge to do justice to her quality, might have become a champion. However, it was not for some years, years during which one disappointment after another provided us with a hard education, that we were first to acquire and then to breed Border Terriers which we were able to campaign to their titles. We have subsequently achieved some success in the breed from a small kennel, which in theory consists of no more than half-a-dozen adult dogs but which, especially in recent years, has very occasionally risen to almost double that number. Far more important than success, we have derived enjoyment both from the dogs which share our home and from the friendship of people, in many parts of the world, who share our regard for the breed. Border Terriers have provided us with sport, competition, companionship, interest, challenges, opportunities and much, much more. They have, quite literally, altered the course of our lives.

We have also reared our own family, both of whom, Simon and Elspeth, now share our interest in the Border Terrier and who, like us, are Championship Show judges of the breed.

As we have said, this book is the product of an enthusiasm which, to those who find it difficult to understand the way in which dogs can enrich life, may seem to approach the obsessive, and as such it is unlikely to offer a balanced assessment. Even so, we have tried to pass on some of what we have learned and especially the enjoyment we have had, and continue to have, from the breed which we regard as very special indeed. And although we hope this book will contain something of interest to those who share our long commitment, its main purpose is to provide encouragement and guidance for newcomers and perhaps even to proselytize. Not that the Border Terrier needs an evangelist: its size, good nature, rugged good looks and relatively undemanding maintenance needs are making it increasingly popular. That, however, is a matter for concern to its long-established supporters. It is currently the eighteenth most popular breed in Britain, and such a situation is not without its dangers – but it would be churlish to attempt to deny others access to all the enjoyment, excitement, companionship, interest, social contact and sport which we have enjoyed for so many years and which we hope to continue to enjoy for many more years to come.

Jean and Frank Jackson
Ashworth Moor
Lancashire
1996

1

The History of the Breed

A number of hunts have, in the past, developed their own particular strains of terrier. The Cheshire, Cottesmore, the Fitzwilliam, Grove, Quorn, Ullswater and several others have all at various times had their own distinct and well known strains, although most have now either disappeared or been subsumed into other breeds. Border Terriers remain a distinctive breed whose name commemorates the name of the hunt, the Border Foxhounds, in which they were developed.

The breed was created in order to carry out a specific and demanding task, to eject foxes from places in which they had taken refuge. It was not created overnight, nor was it created in order to satisfy the vision of a particular individual. The control of foxes in that part of the Cheviots hunted by the Border Foxhounds and its predecessors needed a particular sort of terrier, and everything about the Border Terrier was, and is, shaped by its original purpose in life.

The terrier stock from which the breed evolved had doubtless existed for many years, and has given rise to other breeds with which the Border Terrier shares some family resemblances. Even today it is not unknown for vestiges of the Dandie Dinmont's topknot to appear, and even a tendency to the Dandie's round eye; and the racy outline and pump-handle tail of the Bedlington Terrier are seen, in less exaggerated form, in some Border Terriers. These three breeds come from the same part of Britain and all probably share a common root stock. The Dandie Dinmont, in its less literary guise of the Pepper and Mustard Terrier, appears to have been used as a general purpose vermin dog while the Bedlington Terrier was developed principally as a rabbiting dog.

De Venatione written by Oppian (Oppianos of Apamea) in AD 207 offers what may well be the first description of terriers and their purpose in life. In 1771 Oppian's work was translated by John Whittaker and published as part of his *The History of Manchester*. These dogs – small, black-eyed, rough-coated, strong-jawed, lean and workmanlike – were to be found among the tribes of 'Britain's wildest shore'. Could this be Northumberland? Did Oppian, nearly 1800 years ago, describe the Border Terrier's ancestors? Unfortunately he fails to identify the 'secret prey' alluded to in his work, nor does he make any reference to 'Aggasses' working below ground. We know only that Aggasses, a word which derives from that used to refer to lowly and hard-working servants, were used to drive a quarry out of its place of refuge and then to follow its scent and kill it.

Hunting in any country where inaccessible places abounded, either in cover or below ground, in which the quarry could take refuge, produced the need for a type of dog capable of driving that quarry out into the open where it might be taken in nets, flown at by hawks and falcons or coursed by hounds. These dogs needed to be small enough and willing to enter these places, with a sufficiently thick coat and pelt to withstand rough wear and tear, also courageous enough to face a far larger foe and determined enough to persuade a reluctant animal to vacate its place of refuge. Quarry likely to hide underground tended to be despised as cowardly and unworthy of attention, and this particularly applied to the fox. Although etymologists invariably reject the possibility, it seems possible that the word 'terrier' derives not from any reference to the earth, but to the simple fact that these small dogs were used to so terrorize their quarry that it took flight.

The Bayeux Tapestry depicts events which took place in 1066 and provides a picture of what the forerunners of modern terriers looked like. In two places it shows Harold accompanied by small, long-legged, coloured dogs with uncut tails. Harold carries a hawk on his gloved fist.

Two hundred years later, foxes were being hunted in Northumberland not principally for sport, but as a means to protect sheep and lambs from their depredations. In 1219 Henry III gave John Fitz-Robert permission *'to keep dogs of his own to hunt foxes and hares in the forest of Northumbria'*. Hunting foxes with hounds in Northumbria would be inconceivable without the services of a useful terrier and so it follows that, from the beginning of the thirteenth century, there must have been terriers in Border country. Obviously these terriers must have conformed to the strict and inviolable standard which work imposes, but we can only guess at what they might have looked like. Almost certainly they would be coloured, with rough, weather-resistant coats; they would be undocked; they would be 'on the leg' so that they could make their way across rough country and stay in touch with horsemen; they would be tough and courageous, and they would also be intelligent and resourceful. More cannot be said with any degree of certainty.

William de Blatherwyke, sometimes called William de Foxhunte, was huntsman to King Edward I and may well have been among the first professional huntsmen whose careers were devoted to hunting fox; his own extended over the last twenty-five years of the thirteenth century. The pack, which variously consisted of '30 fox-dogs' or '14 running dogs', hunted 'in divers forest and parks for foxes' throughout the year. Its purpose appears not to have been to provide sport, but simply to furnish the court with a regular supply of good quality fox pelts, and for this reason the hunt's expenses were charged to the keeper of the royal wardrobe.

Foxes became upwardly mobile as a quarry during the reign of Edward II, whose huntsmen, William Twiti and his successor Alan de Leek, had their activities confined to a season which lasted 'fra the Nativyte tyll the annunciation of owre lady fre', from 8 September until 25 March; this suggests that foxes were no longer regarded as vermin to be slaughtered by any means at any time.

During the 1570s a number of descriptions of terriers, and of the way in which they were employed in Britain, were published. The first was the Latin text of Dr Johannes Caius, *De Canibus Britannicus*, published independently in 1570. In 1576 Abraham Fleming published, under the title *Of Englishe Dogges*, what purported to be a translation but which diverged so much from the original that, in our view, it is best regarded as an original work. Fleming's *opus* contained the now-familiar description of terrier work:

Of the Dogge called Terrar, in Latine *Terrarius*.

> Another sorte there is which hunteth the Foxe and the Badger or Greye onely, whom we call Terrars, because they (after the maner and custome of ferrets in searching for Connyes) creepe into the grounde, and by that means make afrayde, nyppe, and byte the Foxe and the Badger in such sort, that eyther they teare them in pieces with theyr teeth beyng in the bosome of the erth, or else hayle and pull them perforce out of their lurking angles, darke dongens, and close caves, or at the least through coceved feare, drive them out of their hollow harbours, in so much that they are compelled to prepare speedy flight, and being desirous of the next (albeit not the safest) refuge, are otherwise taken and intrapped with snares and nettes layde over holes to the same purpose. But these be the least in that kynde called *Sagax*.

11

Compare Fleming's wordy description with an accurate translation of Caius' Latin original:

> Some are Fox and Badger Hounds only: called the *Terrarii* because they penetrate holes in the earth, as ferrets do when after rabbits, and so frighten and bite the fox and the badger that they either tear them on the ground with their teeth, or force them from their lairs into flight or into nets drawn over the burrows in the ground. These form the smallest class of Sagaces.

Also published in 1576 was George Turbervile's *The Noble Arte of Venerie or Hunting*. In all but name and a few additional comments, this was a translation of the Count Jacques du Fouilloux's French original *La Venerie*, which had been published in 1561, and so perhaps should not be relied on too heavily as evidence of British practice. Nevertheless the description of what was then the process of entering a terrier is not without interest:

> Now to speake of Fox houndes and Terryers, and how you should enter them to take the Foxe, the Badgerd, and suche like vermin: whereof you muste understand that ther are sundrie sortes of Terriers, whereof wee hold opinion that one sorte came out of Flaunders or the low Countries, as Artoys and thereabouts, and they have crooked legges, and are shorte heared moste commonly. Another sorte there is which are shagged and streight legged: those with the crooked legges will take earth better than the other, and are better for the Badgerd, bycause they will lye longer at a vermine: but the others with streight legges do serve for twoo purposes, for they wyll Hunte above the grounde as well as other houndes, and enter the earthe with more furie than the others: but they will not abide so long, bycause they are too eagre in fight, and therefore are constreyned to come out to take the ayre: there are both good and badde of bothe sortes. And bycause it is good pastime, and brave fight, without great payne or travayle to the huntsman, therefore I have thought good to set downe here some preceptes for the entryng of Terriers, and for the better fleshyng and encouraging of them.
> You shall beginne to enter them as soone as they be eyght or tenne moneths old: for if you enter not a Terrier before he be a yeare old, you shall hardly make him take the earth. And you must take goode heede that you encourage them, and rebuke them not at the firste: nor that the Foxe or Badgerd do hurt them within the earth, for then they will never love the earth agayne. And therefore never enter a yong Terryer in an earth where there is an olde Foxe or Badgerd: But first lette them be well entred, and be a yeare old full or more. You shall do well also to put an

old Terryer before them which may abide and endure the furie of the Foxe or Badgerd. You may enter them and fleshe them sundrie wayes. First when Foxes and Badgerds have yong cubbes, take all your olde Terryers and put then into the grounde: and when they beginne to baye (which in the earth is called yearning), you muste holde your yong Terryers every one of them at a sundrie hole of some angle or mouth of the earth, that they may herken and heare theyr fellowes yearne. And when you have taken the old Foxes and Badgerdes, and that there is nothing left in the earth but the yong Cubbes, take out then all your old Terryers, and couple them, crying, To him, To him, To him; and if they take any yong Cubbe, lette them take theyr pleasure of him, and kill him within the grounde: and beware that the earth fall not downe upon them and smoother them. That done, take all the rest of the Cubbes and Badgerds pigges home with you, and frie theyr livers and theyr bloud with cheese, and some of theyr owne greace, and thereof make your Terryers a rewarde, shewying them always the heads and skinnes to encourage them. When they have bene rewarded or rather before, washe them with Sope and warme water to get out the clay which shall be clodded in theyr heare: for els they will soone become mangie: and that would be harde to be cured.

He that will be present at such pastimes, may do well to be booted: For I have lent a Foxe or a Badgerd ere nowe, a piece of my hose, and the skyn and fleshe for companie, which he never restored agayne.'

Let these few precepts suffise for the hunting of Foxes and Badgerds.

John Leslie's *De origine, moribus, et rebus gestis Acotorum* was published two years later in 1578 and subsequently translated into English as the *History of Scotland*. It contains a reference to:

a dog of low height indeed, but of bulkier body; which, creeping into subterraneous burrows, routs out the foxes, badgers, martens, and wild cats from their lurking-places and dens. He, if he at any time finds the passage too narrow, opens himself a way with his feet, and that with so great labour that he frequently perishes through his own exertions.

Fouilloux and Caius probably wrote original works, though Caius might have referred to Fouilloux; but Fleming, Turbervile and Leslie, style apart, added little of importance to the canon. Even so, together they demonstrate that terriers were an integral part of hunting towards the end of the sixteenth century and that terrier work was carefully regulated.

It is not until the mid-eighteenth century that pictorial proof becomes available of the existence of terriers which could take their place among modern Border Terriers without looking out of place. A painting was commissioned by William Tufnell Joliffe from Nathaniel Drake (1727–1778) which has become an integral part of Border Terrier history. The painting dates from some time prior to 1765, when Joliffe gave up his hounds. It shows old Arthur Wentworth, earthstopper to the Tufnell Joliffe hounds, mounted on a rugged old pony and well wrapped against the cold of a winter night, armed with spade and mattock and with two terriers at his pony's feet: one is red, the other blue and tan, and both are of the same breed – on the leg and moderately long-backed, with hound-like shoulders, strong loins, racy hindquarters, thick, undocked tails and broad heads. If they are not Border Terriers they are certainly of the stock from which Border Terriers descended. The painting was subsequently published as a print in three different versions which appeared in 1767, 1794 and, in William Daniel's *Rural Sports*, in 1807.

Arthur Wentworth was born round about 1690, but where remains a mystery. He saw service as an earthstopper with the Earl of Carlisle's hounds, with Henry Brewster Darley's hounds and, at the age of seventy-five, was in service with Tufnell Joliffe and Mann Horsefield. During the later stages of his long career he lived at Bulmer, Castle Howard, Yorkshire.

The Earl of Carlisle was probably associated with the Old Cumberland and Inglewood Hunts, or their predecessors; these were amalgamated in 1827 to form the Cumberland. They hunted countries in the western Border counties, and it seems probable that Arthur Wentworth's terriers and possibly Wentworth himself came from the Borders. Tufnell Joliffe's hounds hunted part of what is now the Holderness country; the amalgamation may have taken place in 1765 when William Bethel created the Holderness in its present form.

At about the same time Thomas Bewick, who lived in Border country, produced a number of engravings which included terriers of a uniform type. The pictorial evidence is supported by the description which appears in his *History of Quadrupeds*, published in 1790:

> The Terrier has a most acute smell, is generally an attendant on every pack of Hounds, and is very expert in forcing Foxes or other game out of their coverts. It is the determined enemy of all the vermin kind; such as Weasels, Foumarts, Badgers, Rats, Mice, etc. It is fierce, keen, and hardy; and in its encounters with the Badger, sometimes meets with very severe treatment, which it sustains with great courage and fortitude. A well-trained Dog frequently proves more than a match for that hard-biting animal.

There are two kinds of Terriers, – the one rough, short-legged, long-backed, very strong, and commonly of a black or yellowish colour, mixed with white; the other is smooth, sleek, and beautifully formed, having a shorter body, and more sprightly appearance: it is generally of a reddish brown colour, or black, with tanned legs; and is similar to the rough Terrier in disposition and faculties, but inferior in size, strength, and hardiness.

There can be no doubt but that during the eighteenth century, Border country contained terriers that were very like our modern Border Terriers. During the next few years the history of the breed contains nothing more substantial than highly romantic tales, often refuted and, as far as we are aware, never verified, which involve the notorious Willie and Jamie Allen, Sir Walter Scott and the saga of Dandie Dinmont. Sir Edwin Landseer, Robert Surtees and even George Borrow are also sometimes given small walk-on parts.

It was only during the eighteenth century and, more especially, during the middle and late years of the nineteenth century that fox-hunting became established as a socially acceptable pastime for fashionable people. They enhanced their appearance by wearing scarlet coats, the most fashionable of which were tailored by the eponymous Thomas Pink, and their concern for appearance gave rise to breeds of white or predominantly white terriers. Where utility and not fashion remained of paramount importance, in Ireland and in the northern counties of England, loyalty to the old grey and green hunt uniforms remained steadfast and the terriers remained true to the old colours of red, tan, wheaten and blue.

In 1781, Peter Beckford's hunting classic *Thoughts on Hunting* had been published. Beckford was MP for Morpeth and so must have had experience of hunting in Border country; nor could he have been unaware of the sort of terriers used in the Border hunt countries. Yet Beckford wrote that 'I should prefer the black or white terrier; some there are so like a fox, that awkward people frequently mistake one for the other.' Prejudice against coloured terriers remains among 'awkward people' who nowadays support their view by accusing hounds of being likely to confuse a coloured terrier with their quarry.

We need to turn to the history of fox-hunting in Northumbria to find more detailed information. Thus, the Kielder hounds were favourably noticed in the early 1800s by that most snobbish of sporting reporters Nimrod. They were hunted by the Robson family who, in 1857, moved the pack to Byrness in Reedwater where they were amalgamated with hounds kept by John Dodd of Catcleugh. The new pack was known as the Reedwater Hounds. In 1869 Jacob's son, John, took over the mastership and the name was changed to the Border Foxhounds. It was within this pack and two neighbouring packs, the Liddesdale and the North Tyne that Border Terriers, as we know them today, were developed. For work with hounds the three packs relied on the white Redesdale Terriers, now extinct, and the coloured Coquetdale Terriers which have, because of their close association with the Border Foxhounds, since become known as Border Terriers.

The terriers of the region first began to appear in the ring when the newly formed Agricultural Societies began to run shows during the last few years of the eighteenth century, long before the idea was first born of running what is often regarded as the first dog show, which took place in Newcastle in 1859. By the time this show took place –consisting of two classes for bitches tagged on to an existing poultry show –shows in the region had been putting on classes for hounds, sheepdogs and terriers for many years.

Attempts to put Border Terriers on a more formal footing were made in 1895 when John Houliston tried to found a club. His attempts came to nothing, as did the first application, made in 1914, for Kennel Club recognition. In 1920, however, the Kennel Club was finally persuaded –by Captain Hamilton Adams, one of its members who bred Sealyhams and lived in Eastbourne –to accept the breed as an old breed which, the captain claimed, was in the process of being revived. Prior to recognition, fears had been expressed that the breed would be ruined as a working terrier because the fashionable demands of the show ring were given priority over more essential matters. In order to prevent this, the newly formed Border Terrier Club drew up its own Standard and that approved by the Kennel Club was quietly scrapped. Even so, not all the breed's supporters were satisfied, and some formed the short-lived Northumberland Border Terrier Club which not only continued to oppose recognition but even went so far as to try to prevent people who did not live in Northumberland from being involved with the breed.

In the year after recognition the popularity of Border Terriers reached a level which it was not to reach again for many years. Perhaps a novelty factor was at work. If it was, then it soon disappeared, and the breed settled down to a comfortable level of popularity which remained remarkably consistent until the mid-1970s.

During the years from 1975 to 2002 the popularity of Border Terriers in Britain, measured as a percentage of total Kennel Club registrations, more than quadrupled. From 0.56 in 1974 they had risen to 2.36 per cent in 2002. Unfortunately popularity brought with it problems that the breed had not previously encountered. These include the attention of puppy farmers, supermarkets and some large, unlicensed, commercial breeding kennels whose concern about hereditary faults, socialization, suitable housing, hygiene and protection from disease may not always be apparent. In the past, 'experts' had either disparaged Border Terriers as lacking the qualities which might lead to popular appeal, or had ignored the breed; it was not regarded as sufficiently glamorous or exotic to achieve popularity. It would be comforting to believe that popularity was achieved because the public recognized qualities which were not apparent to the 'experts'. In fact it seems more likely that popularity has risen as other breeds have revealed or developed faults which have made them less popular. It may also be that during the last twenty years a few large kennels have begun to breed and market puppies in a way which had not previously happened. Herein may be the seeds of the breed's fall from its present popularity.

By the mid-1920s the two societies had pooled their resources and produced a Standard which, after a period during which minor refinements were made, was to remain virtually unchanged until, in 1986, the Kennel Club insisted on changes being made for the sake of editorial uniformity. Fortunately the Kennel Club was prepared to heed the advice of individuals with a knowledge of the breed, principally W. Ronald Irving and Frank Jackson, and so narrowly avoided the introduction of ill-advised and potentially damaging material changes.

2

Purpose

Although Border Terriers have been employed on a variety of quarry, both legitimate and illegitimate, the breed was brought into being principally to work alongside hounds and to play its part in hunting foxes. To understand it, it is necessary to appreciate the demands made on its physique and temperament by the work it was evolved to do. Regrettably few of the breed's supporters fully understand what is expected of a terrier working with foxhounds in the Border counties. Some take doubtless thoroughly justified pride in their terrier's prowess with rabbits, rats, mink, weasels, stoats, grey squirrels and even moorhens, and in the past Border Terriers were tested against badgers, otters, wild cats and coypu. Overseas, tests of working ability were provided by woodchuck, coyote, raccoon and other assorted ground quarry. It must, however, be stressed that none of these activities were influential in the development of the Border Terrier. Even work to fox cannot really be regarded as totally relevant unless carried out in association with hounds and in countries which impose precisely the same demands as does the inhospitable moorland which forms most of the Border country.

Early 1995 saw renewed and determined efforts in Parliament to pass a Bill which would ban all forms of hunting with hounds or terriers. We do not intend to discuss the rights or wrongs of the Bill or its probable successors, but its existence does provide evidence of a determination to bring to an end field sports which employ hounds and terriers. The Bill may, to some-extent at least, have been provoked by a spate of damaging, albeit not always accurately reported, publicity during the late 1980s. This was the product of injudicious or illegal work with terriers coupled with a determination among some people to present hunting in the worst possible light. In response, the Masters of Foxhounds Association drew up a Code of Good Hunting Practice. Much of the Code was devoted to practices which, it is to be hoped, would have been observed as a matter of course by all courteous folk who understood country ways – but not for the first time, hunting again found it necessary to legislate for the behaviour of Beckford's *awkward people*. Only a small part of the Code addressed problems which may arise as a consequence of terrier work:

> If when a fox is run to ground, the decision is that it be killed, it is usually necessary to use terriers. The terrierman charged with the duty of humanely destroying the fox should normally be accompanied by one assistant only and every effort should be made to discourage the presence of foot followers and members of the general public.
>
> Terriermen, whether or not directly employed by the hunt, are to be regarded as hunt servants; they must be aware of the provisions of the Rules and of this Code.

The Masters Association also sought to support their Code by asking Masters not to make indiscriminate use of terriers belonging to local enthusiasts and to refrain from issuing working certificates. The request was ignored by some hunts, and some breed clubs also failed to support the Masters Association by continuing to issue working certificates.

The threat to the opportunity for Border Terriers to continue to work under genuine conditions is obvious. Even fewer people than previously would have the opportunity to test their terriers in the traditional way, or even to see terriers working in the manner which was responsible for shaping the Border Terrier characteristics. It thus becomes even more important that Border Terrier owners understand just what the breed was developed to do. Once more we record, but refrain from judging. In fact the opening sentence in the Breed Standard says it all: **The Border Terrier is essentially a working terrier**. . . Moreover there are only two requirements sought by the Breed Standard which are not relevant to work, namely dark eyes and a short, gaily carried tail. Everything else contributes to the ability to work or to endure the conditions in which work takes place.

In 1927 George Thompson, then Secretary of the Border Terrier Club, wrote a chapter on the breed for C.C. Sanderson's *Pedigree Dogs*; in it, he expressed what can fairly be regarded as what was then the Club's attitude to the breed:

> It is purely a 'working terrier' and it is known to many that for generations Border farmers, shepherds and sportsmen carefully preserved a particular strain of terrier which could be found in almost every Border homestead.

With the hills at their disposal and miles from habitation, stock were subjected to the ravages of the big and powerful hill foxes, and the Border farmer and shepherd required a dead game terrier to hunt and kill them, with length of leg sufficient to follow a horse, yet small enough to follow a fox to ground.

These terriers had naturally to be active, strong and tireless, and to have sound, weather-resisting coats in order to withstand prolonged exposure to drenching rains and mists in the hills. He is the most tireless hard-worker for his size, and full of pluck; there is no wall he cannot get over or wire entanglement he is unable to scramble through; should the fox run to earth he will bolt him every time, or stay the night in the earth until the matter is settled from his point of view.

The sentiments expressed on behalf of the Border Terrier Club by George Thompson remain every bit as valid nearly seventy years later, though whether every exhibitor and judge shows them the respect which is their due is perhaps uncertain.

The Border Terrier and the Parson Jack Russell Terrier are the only recognized British terrier breeds which have retained strong and close links with the purpose for which they were originally developed. Certainly the Border Terrier's appearance and character are almost entirely the product of the work it has always been asked to do, and to understand the breed it is essential to know at least something about its purpose. This purpose it shares nowadays with the working Lakeland Terrier, a dog very different from the breed we admire in the ring, the Fell Terrier, often referred to as the Patterdale Terrier and the old-fashioned Parson Jack Russell Terrier. All these terriers were developed in different parts of Britain to run with hounds hunting wild and difficult terrain, and to be at hand to eject foxes from any places in which they might happen to seek refuge. All these breeds were developed exclusively to work to fox in a particular way.

All are rightly wary of the possible effects of Kennel Club recognition, for fear that a career in the show ring might result in changes which would destroy their value as working terriers. The Border Terrier was the first to accept the risk, the Parson Jack Russell did so recently, and the rest continue to withstand the temptation, though both breeds still contain a number of determined breeders who remain convinced that recognition is the gateway to the road to ruin.

One need only look at other breeds, not confined to the terrier group, to realize that their fears are not unreasonable. Nor is the struggle to retain contact with work – however precarious – and to maintain respect for its demands ever likely to be won. It is a struggle which must be continually waged by breeders, exhibitors and by judges; all have a responsibility to maintain a type suitable for work, and to do so they must have a firm appreciation of what that work entails. Right, however, is not concentrated on one side. People whose prime interest is in the show ring may be tempted to disregard working qualities, but some of those whose primary interest is in work seem almost to take a perverse delight in owning terriers which are handsome only in as far as handsome does. They take the easy way out, and by doing so pose a threat to the breed. If Masters were to take a similar attitude towards their hounds, packs would consist of a motley collection of nondescripts pleasing to neither eye nor ear. That they have not done so has resulted in the Foxhound being one of the finest examples of the breeder's art, combining superb hunting ability with beauty and melody. If *all* Border Terrier breeders would only adopt a similar attitude, the breed's future as an attractive working terrier would be assured.

What then does this work consist of? Hunting takes place in winter, traditionally starting on 1 November, though cubbing may begin as soon as cereal crops are harvested. As far as Border Terriers are concerned, hunting takes place among the fells and moors of Northumbria, in a part of the country where the geography and winter climate are very much less hospitable than its people. The conditions are often such as to give support to Doctor Samuel Johnson's view that 'only the paucity of human pleasures convinces us that hunting is one of them'.

Hunting is not, however, merely a fashionable winter sport: it remains the most effective, and arguably the least cruel, means of controlling the foxes which would otherwise play havoc with the sheep on which the farmers of the region rely for their livelihood. Traditionally hounds were kept in ones and twos at farmsteads in the area, being brought to the meet by their owners or summoned by the huntsman's horn. Nowadays most, if not all, the packs kennel their hounds together. Terriers may be either in the ownership of hunt followers or be owned by the hunt itself.

The pack meets at an appointed place, and is then taken to draw where a fox or foxes are thought to be in residence. Border Terriers share the task and are expected to work in much the same way as did their predecessors hundreds of years ago: their small size, thick skins and double, impervious coats, their courage, determination and resourcefulness enable them to search dense undergrowth which

21

might be impenetrable to a foxhound. The terriers used by William I almost a thousand years ago worked in just this way to drive quarry, in those days deer or birds, from dense places of refuge so that it could be taken in nets, coursed by hounds or flown at by hawks.

Once a fox has been found it will attempt to make its escape, and the traditional British spectacle, encapsulated by Oscar Wilde of 'the English country gentleman galloping after a fox – the unspeakable in full pursuit of the uneatable' now unfolds. In all likelihood the fox will attempt to make his way to distant earths where he knows hounds cannot reach him.

There is a marvellously evocative description in T. Scott Anderson's *Hound and Horn in Jedforest*; the author was Master of the Jedforest from 1892 to 1934:

> Some of the Hounds may become separated from the followers toiling along in their wake, while the terriers which run with them use all their wiles to ensure that they are at hand to follow any fox which may happen to go to ground. They must be capable of ejecting him from any place in which he might seek refuge. From deep moss holes, from narrow cracks between immoveable rocks, from among labyrinths formed by tree roots and from narrow drains.

Border terriers normally enjoy an amicable relationship with one another.

In what way have the demands imposed by this work influenced the breed's development? It is, in the first place, apparent that a Border Terrier must be capable of working amicably with hounds, with other terriers, with people and among farm stock. A sociable and steady disposition is therefore of paramount importance, and the so-called 'terrier spirit' which produces a hysterically aggressive fiend is not something which could ever be tolerated in any terrier which is expected to work for his living. A Border Terrier must have the speed, agility and stamina to stay with hounds, not just through the course of a long day's hunting on the fells, but several days a week throughout a long and arduous season. Of course, in a race over a straight course no Border Terrier could possibly match the speed of a Foxhound and would be left trailing in the wake of a galloping horse; so in order to stay in contact with hounds they will cut corners, anticipate where Charley may be heading, use their prior knowledge of the country and allow no obstacle to prevent them achieving their objective. To do this, their physical attributes, freedom of movement and stamina must be allied to intelligence and resourcefulness. Moreover, having reached the place in which the fox has taken refuge, they need the courage and the build which will enable them to follow and engage with a formidable quarry, often bigger than they are, which is fighting for its very life.

These foxes untainted by the imports of smaller French foxes that took place during the nineteenth century to ensure that more fashionable hunting countries could be certain of sport, are narrow, rangy, lithe and strong. This is especially true of the Northern hill foxes, and this sort is a truly formidable opponent for any terrier. Yet it is the terrier's task to follow wherever his quarry may lead; across country and then underground, through narrow apertures, through icy mud and water, down steep drops and up difficult climbs – and all in Stygian darkness and an atmosphere pervaded with the musk of successive generations of foxes. In such a situation the terrior must rely entirely on his own resources: if he is too big; if he lacks the agility and flexibility not only to follow his fox but, when his job is done, to retrace his steps; and finally if he lacks the strength and courage to persuade his fox to move – if he fails in any of these he will be of little use and will be quickly discarded.

So, we have tried to explain what a terrier's work entails, and have laid considerable stress on its importance; but we would like to point out that although the explanation is ours, the emphasis derives entirely from the Breed Standard which has *always* unequivocally stated that 'the Border Terrier is essentially a working terrier'. It does not say *'may* be a working terrier', nor does it even say that the Border Terrier *should* be a working terrier': it says it is **'essentially a working terrier'**. Even the most recent changes imposed on the Standard by the Kennel Club have not weakened the requirement, but have strengthened it. The clause which appears at the end of every breed standard – 'any departure from the foregoing points should be considered a fault and the seriousness with which the fault should be regarded should be in exact proportion to its degree' – has been further strengthened in the Border Terrier Standard by adding the words: 'and its effect on the terrier's ability to work'. The breed was grateful for the way in which the Kennel Club recognized the importance of work.

Thus we have established that the temperament and physical ability of the Border Terrier to carry out the task for which the breed was originally developed is of paramount importance; and it must also be the basis for every decision taken in the show-ring. Breed clubs continue to provide classes at their shows for terriers holding working certificates, and it is a matter for regret that they are seldom well supported by terriers which could hope for success in other classes. The real value of working certificates has long been a source for debate.

Writing in the October 1912 issue of *The Foxhound*, Arthur Blake Heinemann expressed what might be regarded as a hypocritical view from someone who was happy to accept Charles Cruft's invitations to judge at his famous show.

Yet to-day it is fashionable to hold classes for working terriers at Dog Shows, and specialize in various breeds or strains, each vying with the other for press-puffs and paragraphs, and capping each others' fairy-tales as to their terrier's exploits; for, tell it not in Gath, this is a profitable game, and as one judge and breeder of the latest candidates for fashion's favour said to me, 'I know they're no use except at home among themselves, but what would you do? I can sell them like hot cakes.' Another judge and breeder of a rival strain also shown of late years, said, 'Be careful when you are buying one, for half of them are no use at all.' 'Deeds, not words' should be the working-terrier's motto, and just as good wine needs no bush, so his record in the Badger-club season's booklet, or the foxes or otters he has bolted for the local packs duly chronicled by the hunting journalist, should prove a better passport to favour than any award at a dog-show, where practical and actual trials are entirely out of the question.

Also it is impossible to judge by appearances, for a dead-game dog may bear a scar, while a more useful and cautious one with tongue may not. I once judged a working-class, of course two ladies were among the competitors, for they dearly love dog shows, and like the late Lord Granville Gordon, I was tempted to give the prize to the best-looking lady; but being out for business, I asked what each terrier had done. Well, one of them had killed twenty moles in one night, and the other was made to sit and beg, when I discovered he was one I had bred and drafted as the ugly duckling of my litter! In this class the terrier I gave first prize to was utterly useless next week to badger, while an unplaced one was the very best a man could wish to work. All of which shows I am a very bad judge; if not, what a farce it all is.

Forbidden fruit is always sweetest, and breeders of show terriers are never tired of dinning into one's ears that their dogs are workers as well, and bred on the right lines for make and shape, but they lose sight of the fact that while they have been breeding them for straightness, they have acquired a giraffe-like length of leg, and while breeding them for appearance and show-points they have lost all their individuality, intelligence and stamina. Pluck, I admit, they still have left them, but it is rare and usually developed in the wrong direction of quarrelsomeness. . . . Buy a show terrier, and do nothing to his coat, and in six months' time you will think your kennelman dishonest, for in the Teddy Bear he leads out for your inspection you will fail to recognise the pin-wire coated champion of Cruft's or the Crystal Palace. Now, breeders of working terriers are bitten with the craze for show-bench honours, and are fast making themselves ridiculous, to say nothing of spoiling the fruits of the labours of long years' breeding . . .

Another time a lady brought down her team of white West Highland terriers, but they would not go to ground, find or bay a badger there, or join in a worry with a dead badger, and she said they didn't like the noise of the diggers shouting, and the noise of their spades and picks, nor the brambles at the mouth of the earth. A third time a youth brought some pretty Dandie-Dinmonts down, and told us yarns about their pluck. These next day would not go to ground, or look at a badger. Noise again! So all mine were kennelled, and in solemn silence a badger let go in view. I regret to say the Dandies wouldn't even hunt his line or go near him. Yet one more, if space admits: Two well-known working terrier men appeared at a big earth very freshly used by badgers. They had a Sealyham with a great reputation. So she went in first to find. 'Nothing there,' said her owner, but there *was*, for he was found by mine, and presently viewed, though not captured, and the Sealyham was found to have a gash on her seat of honour!!! But I am treading on good fellows' corns, and certainly on delicate ground; but a pound of practice is worth a ton of theory.

In 1954 Montague H. Horn, whose little book *The Border Terrier* is a treasured possession of those fortunate enough to own this rare publication, wrote 'On the Working-Terrier Class' for *Our Dogs*. His views are humorously presented but might fairly be regarded as sincere:

> Now let us drop in to that old country inn which has such an ancient link with the chase that it was called 'Ye Olde Fox and Hounds' in the village of Northotine. Of course like many others it has fallen on evil days, but there are still many of us who can recall the rent dinners which used to be held in the 'Longroom' as it was called, where many a welkin has been rung or as Shakespeare said, 'the night owl raised with a catch'. No longer is the hunger of the casual visitor assuaged by ham and eggs followed by apple-pie and cream for a mere half-crown. In fact the long room is now a Cocktail Lounge, presided over by a slim young man whose sole offer of food is a packet of potato-crisps. In place of the engraving 'September Morn' which hung over the fireplace, there is now a dart board of course, and to make room for the television set, they have removed the mask of the dog fox inscribed 'Coltchesters, 1909, 8½ hours'.
>
> Still memories of the old place linger and even tonight, as though an echo of the past, a Border Terrier lies curled asleep before the silent glow of an electric fire. The dog looks as though sitting before a fire of some sort was the main occupation of its little day, and its owner is sitting with the second huntsman of the West Horsley.
>
> After a lengthy whispered conversation, a short sentence on a slip of paper is signed, and the deed is done, the little dog has now procured a working certificate. Another glass is filled, an eye winks!
>
> It has been a long, cold, miserable day with the rain ceasing for only short intervals, and it has been a blank day too. Hounds have travelled a long way beside the rising river, but at last the master calls a halt at the bridge, and among the few who have remained with him until the end is a young woman, leading a weary little Border Terrier.
>
> The master leans upon his pole and tells her that he is sorry sport has been poor, he would have liked to have tried her terrier. He tells her it looks game, and sticking his pole into the sodden ground he runs his hand down its back, spans it behind the shoulders, its head in the palm of his hand, just like judges do in a show ring.
>
> He remarks what is very obvious, that the dog has a grand head, and she informs him that it is a very noted winner, and she says how sorry she is that neither she nor her dog can join them on the North Heddon, where hounds meet on Saturday. Well, it's not his fault that it was a wet day, but he's a decent chap, and has to overcome a lot of worries himself, so he draws a capacious wallet from his pocket and

scribbles a few lines on the back of an old envelope and hands them to the girl. Reading them, she smiles. 'How awfully nice of you,' she says.

'Not at all,' he replies, 'it has been a great honour to meet such a famous little dog. I hope your luck continues.' The little dog picks his way behind his owner's heels, through the wet grass, now eligible for the class for exhibits holding a working certificate.

The desire to protect working ability is no less strong in the United States than in Britain, but very different criteria prevail. There is no widespread tradition of fox-hunting. Even the foxes are said to occasionally demonstrate their contempt for tradition by taking refuge up trees! Working ability has always been at the top of the Border Terrier Club of America's priorities, and in 1994 its importance was recognized by the American Kennel Club. In January, 1994 draft conditions were published for what were referred to as Den Tests – that is, tests intended to provide the means by which aptitude for work below ground could be assessed.

Artificial tests are, at best, but a poor substitute for the real thing, but many might feel they are far better than no test at all. It is very easy to disparage or find fault with artificial working tests, but in the absence of the real things it is very difficult to propose an alternative way of testing working aptitude. Some terrier breeds have taken a quite different course, and now regard the qualities needed in a working terrier as unimportant. If that is their choice it is not for us even to attempt to persuade them that their choice is the wrong one. We would, however, be deeply troubled if Border Terrier enthusiasts were to turn their backs on the reasons for the breed's very existence. Certainly the American Kennel Club's view that *dogs should be bred with their original function in mind* is a view which can only be applauded.

The tests envisaged by the AKC included an Introduction to Quarry, a Junior Earthdog Test, a Senior Earthdog Test and a Master Earthdog Test, in ascending order of severity. The introductory test envisaged a den – poor choice of word, but never mind – occupied by either a caged rat or an artificial quarry properly scented and capable of being moved in order to simulate response to the terrier's presence, and approached by a standard square tunnel approximately 9in (23cm) square, about 10ft (3m) long and with one 90-degree turn. The examinee is released at least 10ft from the mouth of the tunnel, may be given a single command, and must then enter the tunnel. Two minutes are then allowed for the dog to begin 'working' the quarry; 'work' must continue for thirty seconds, and is defined as digging, barking, growling, lunging and biting at the quarry or any other action which, in the judge's opinion, indicates that the dog is attempting to attack it.

Junior and senior tests make sterner demands, including a longer and more complex tunnel, shorter time to begin 'working' and prolonged duration of 'work', until the ultimate test for the title of Master Earthdog is arrived at.

The Master Earthdog Test, like the Senior Earthdog Test, utilizes a 9in square tunnel 30ft (9m) in length with at least three 90-degree turns, and a 4ft (120cm) long side tunnel with no exit but baited with scented straw or grass. The 'den' entrance is hidden and blocked, an unscented false entrance is located about 5ft (1.5m) away, and there is a scent trail at least 20ft (6m) long leading to the entrance to the 'real' den. A mound of earth obscures but does not obstruct the mouth of the real tunnel. Dogs, working in pairs, are released about 100ft (30m) away from the entrances, and must indicate the entrance to the real tunnel entrance before the judge can reach it. The obstruction is then removed and the dog under test is expected to enter, the second dog being secured approximately 10ft from the tunnel entrance. Once in the tunnel, the terrier is expected to negotiate an 18in (46cm) long constriction 5ft (1.5m) from the entrance which reduces the tunnel's width to 6in (15cm). Having negotiated a further obstruction, the terrier is expected to reach the quarry within ninety seconds and to work it for thirty seconds. The judge then attempts to distract the dog by lightly striking the den with a piece of wood. If the dog ignores this distraction it becomes entitled to the title of Master Earthdog.

Criticism of these tests should not in any way be regarded as criticism of their excellent intentions, but they do appear to have been devised by people with little knowledge of what is expected of a genuine working terrier, of the conditions it might face underground or, indeed, of what might be regarded as evidence of working aptitude. Indeed, it could be argued that a terrier which performs well in these tests might be well on the way towards being ruined for real work.

A working terrier must be trustworthy among hounds and terriers as well as among farm stock, and must accept perfunctory handling from strangers. A sensible terrier, like an experienced boxer, will not rush into the fray before the opposition has been assessed, and so may take longer than a mere fifteen seconds before going to ground. Once below ground the conditions may be far less comfortable and certainly far less capacious than those provided by any of the artificial tunnels.

An eminently collectable drawing by Vernon Stokes of Border terriers with Otterhounds.

The task of a terrier working with hounds is to persuade his quarry to vacate the premises, using what the constabulary refers to as 'the minimum necessary force'; driving in to attack, lunging and biting are not encouraged. On the other hand a terrier used as a destroyer of vermin was, and is, certainly expected to be capable of destroying his quarry – but whenever did a mere killer of vermin earn a working certificate? In our view, terriers which have successfully satisfied the demands of the AKC Master Earthdog Test would almost certainly have been ruined for the sort of tasks which Border Terriers were traditionally bred to perform, and although their aptitude would have been tested to some degree, their temperament, courage, stamina, intelligence and ability to negotiate very restricted places would not have been tested at all. Even so, we must repeat that these tests are far better than nothing.

No terrier can be forced to work. Efforts to push a terrier into an earth, perhaps in order to convince a compliant and none-too-scrupulous Master to sign a working certificate may achieve its objective, but it will not create a working terrier. Border Terriers perhaps need a more careful introduction to work than some other breeds which even at six or seven months old will rush headlong into an earth without thought for the consequences. Border Terriers tend to give the matter more thought, and for this reason may be discarded as useless by owners accustomed to the headlong dash of other breeds, or who themselves lack the patience and understanding to respect this more cautious approach.

Many Border Terrier breeders furnish puppy runs and exercise areas with pipes and tunnels: these help to introduce youngsters to new experiences and so further the important process of socialization, and also serve to accustom them to entering the sort of restricted, dark places they will encounter when they are introduced to work.

A country walk may, with the permission of the landowner, also provide opportunities for youngsters to investigate holes and tunnels, although care must be taken to ensure that none of these are occupied badger setts, and that the experience respects the hunting season. Nor should any terrier ever be encouraged to go underground unless the owner has the means to effect a rescue should it be unable to get out again. Far too often owners allow or even encourage a terrier to follow its instincts, only to find that it fails to return. The owner may then face a need to explain himself to the police, the terrier is in jeopardy, and effecting a rescue may be a protracted and costly business. Some owners may afterwards boast of what is, in effect, their negligence and ignorance. They do not, however, impress those who understand the breed, know about work, or respect country conventions.

An old friend of ours was wont to talk a good fight as far as Borders were concerned: digging a hole in the rose bed, chasing cats, killing fowl, attempting to catch flies were all regarded as evidence that the kennel contained genuine working Border Terriers. One day, however, the ultimate proof became available: a bitch had gone missing, and according to its owner, had undoubtedly gone to ground. Here was proof positive of the kennel's working attributes. The owner seemed blithely unaware that anyone who allows a Border to wander off, perhaps to go to ground in an unknown place from which it cannot escape without aid, can have little genuine concern for the welfare of their Borders.

Herbaceous border!

Several local Border folk were recruited to search for the errant terrier. All the local earths and setts were investigated; the police, rescue organizations, veterinary surgeons and every likely refuge were interrogated without result. Then some days later, when hope was beginning to fade, a call came from a local hospital to say that a little brown dog had been rescued from the roof. Apparently it must have chased a cat up the fire escape and been unable to retrace its steps. The tale of the 'working Border Terrier' rescued from a hospital roof provided enjoyment for months, and resulted in the kennel making fewer claims about 'work'.

As well as a readiness to go below ground, any terrier used for work must be capable of getting on well with other terriers and with their owners. If it is expected to work above ground, by drawing cover or by running with hounds, it must be absolutely trustworthy with all forms of farm stock, a requirement which is totally ignored by breed club working certificates and by artificial tests; yet it is one which might easily be tested.

The Wild Mammals (Protection) Act 1996 makes it an offence to mutilate, kick, beat, nail, impale, stab, burn, stone, crush, drown, drag or asphyxiate any wild animal with intent to cause unnecessary suffering. The act contains five exclusions which may be intended to protect field sports from mischievous legal harassment while not in any way eroding the protection which the Act offers to wild mammals.

It is not an offence to kill or attempt to kill a fatally disabled wild mammal as an act of mercy. Nor is the reasonable, humane and swift dispatch of a wild mammal injured or taken as a result of shooting an offence. The following activities are not regarded as offences, either: actions authorized by statute; the use of poisonous or noxious substances sanctioned by law; and any action unlawful under the act using snare, trap, dog or bird *if that action* is carried out lawfully for the purpose of killing or taking any wild mammal. However, anyone who ventures onto private land without permission, or whose terrier does so are very likely to find themselves on the wrong side of the law and especially so if the terrier goes to ground or in any way disturbs farm livestock.

Finally, may we alert judges to the possibility that Borders with supposedly 'honourable' scars may have acquired these in ways which are far from honourable in order to pull the wool over the eyes of gullible judges. Work is important to the breed, but it must be legitimate work, and this involves a Border running with hounds and

31

going to ground to fox. In order to preserve the quality of working Border Terriers they must be obliged to compete with all other Border Terriers, and should not be protected from open competition by a working certificate, no matter how reliable it may be.

3

The Breed Standard

Every decision taken in the show ring must rely on the guidance provided by the Breed Standard. The Standard is the product of a process of synthesis and development which began during the early years of this century, leading to that produced by the Border Terrier Club when the breed was first recognized in 1920. The process of refinement continued until the mid-1920s, by which time it was fairly established; it was to remain unchanged until 1986. The changes imposed by the Kennel Club have not materially affected the Standard which had served the breed so well, but the process of editing,

730   THE ILLUSTRATED KENNEL·NEWS.   DECEMBER 12, 1913.

Mr. W. BARTON'S Border Terriers,

at Whitrope, Newcastleton, Roxburghshire.

IN the wild, hilly country on the borders of Scotland and England this but too little known dog has his native home, as his name implies. Here this grand little fellow is appreciated at his true worth, and only needs to be better known in the canine world beyond to become one of the most popular Terriers in the universe, as he is, beyond dispute, the gamest and pluckiest. A small, alert, game-looking dog, 12 to 13 inches from the ground to top of shoulder, between 14 and 16 lbs. weight, with coat of thick-set, hard hair of a dark red colour, rather short in head, but of good width,

of her breed; her record on the show bench is unbeaten, and this year at Langholm she had the distinction of winning the silver challenge cup presented by Miss Mary Rew, the first ever offered for the breed at any show. Nailer, one of her kennel mates, is a great little dog, whose show career is equally good, but it is on the hillside he is seen at his best, where he promises to rival the prowess of his ill-fated sire Rock, whose gameness cost him his life when hunting with the Liddesdale Hounds. Mr. Barton has espoused their cause for many years, and owns the largest and most successful kennel in

run to ground in a moss hole. Bess entered, and after a severe fight, in which she got badly bitten, bolted her fox, who again holed a few miles further on. Another Terrier was entered, who made a game attempt, but failed to dislodge Reynard. Bess again went in, closed with the fox, and fought him for two hours before bolting him, and when he appeared she was hanging on to him. On another occasion, when crossing a linn, she marked an otter amongst some large boulders, and after a struggle, in which she again got badly bitten, she bolted him. A Foxhound who accompanied Mr.

Photos by]   *[J. E. D. Murray, Hawick.*

NAILER.   NAILER AND VENUS.   VENUS.

powerful jaw, small dark eye, with ears hanging more like those of a Foxhound than a Fox Terrier, narrow in shoulder, straight in leg, and small, round feet, with that "fear-no-foe" expression which stamps him as a Terrier beyond ordinary. This is no chance breed of a nondescript character, but has been bred and kept pure by the Border sportsmen for generations, and breeds as true to type as any of the better-known Terriers. Classes are generally given for the breed at the Border shows, and here Mr. Barton's splendid team has always proved invincible. In the bitch Venus, whose photo we reproduce, Mr. Barton owns the acknowledged best

the kingdom, not only on the show bench but in the realm of sport. In this wild country so many strongholds abound in which foxes take refuge when hunted, that without good Terriers fox-hunting would be impossible. These holes are generally either wet moss holes, often of great length, or slits in the rocks, sometimes 20 to 30 feet in depth. These are very dangerous, and to be of any use a Terrier must be small, active, hardy, with a good nose, and courage above suspicion, and in the Border Terrier these qualities are combined to perfection. Mr. Barton's bitch Bess (now thirteen years old), the dam of Venus, already mentioned, is one of the gamest that ever faced a fox. On one occasion when hunting with the Liddesdale pack a fox was

Barton was laid on, and between them the quarry was hunted up and down stream, Bess putting in some grand work in the deep pools, marking every dive the otter made, forcing him to dive or leave the water. He was eventually cornered, and Bess, watching her chance, closed with him, getting him by the throat, and hung on till he was dead. He proved to be a dog otter of 22 lbs. weight. Many similar incidents I could narrate did space permit, but these may serve to prove to the world of sport the existence and value of a dog whose equal for sterling pluck, gameness and determination has yet to be found; and I hope the day is not far distant when he will receive that recognition which he so richly deserves.   CAPSIC.

Willie Barton's kennel.

regarded as necessary to reduce its length (although it was already shorter than any other) has resulted in the omission of some important phrases, regarded as repetitive, and certain words in order to comply with normal standards of English usage.

What can be regarded as the first attempt at producing a Breed Standard was published in *Our Dogs* in 1909. Since the author was none other that Jacob Robson, the description must carry some weight. Then in 1913 *The Illustrated Kennel News* published a revised Standard which, omitting the comparison with Irish Terriers, had the support of Willie Barton who used it in his advertisements. In 1915 Fred Morris produced his own Standard which he claimed had been written with the help of some of the breed's old supporters, although he did not identify them.

Recognition included Kennel Club acceptance of a Breed Standard apparently written by Hamilton Adams, although this was without consultation with, or even the knowledge of existing breeders. Consequently the Standard did not have the breed's support, and was immediately scrapped in favour of one produced in 1920 by the Border Terrier Club.

Thomas Hamilton Adams was a noted breeder of Sealyhams and a member of the Kennel Club; he lived in Eastbourne. His major claim to fame appears to be that in about 1913 he and Major Harry Jones created a kennel of Sealyhams which produced the famous Ch. Ivo Caradoc by The Model out of Ivo Charity, the first and only Sealyham to carry Hamilton Adams' Ivo affix; after gaining his title he almost immediately went to America. Two champion and one CC winning Borders carried the Ivo affix, although they were not bred by Hamilton Adams: they were Ch. Ivo Roisterer (1915) and Ch. Ivo Rarebit (1930) and Ivo Rally. Adams judged the breed at the Crystal Palace in 1922, at Birmingham in 1924, again at Crystal Palace in 1927, the National Terrier in 1929, Richmond in 1932, National Terrier in 1933 and finally again in 1938.

Hamilton Adams' Breed Standard is an accurate description of Ivo Roisterer and has several references to the then Sealyham Terrier Standard. The use of Fox Terriers, then one of the most popular breeds, as some sort of touchstone was probably inevitable, although the deep ribs of both Sealyham and Fox Terrier are a feature not desirable in Border Terriers.

In 1921 the short-lived Northumberland Border Terrier Club was formed after recognition; however, it was not only opposed to the original club, it even went so far as to exclude from its own membership

*Thomas Hamilton Adams's
Ch. Ivo Roisterer. (Photo.
Thomas Fall.)*

anyone who lived outside Northumberland. Even so, this particular Standard was produced by people who knew the breed well, and it would be wrong to ignore it – especially since it was eventually combined with the Border Terrier Club's Standard to produce, after a period of refinement and improvement, what was in effect the final version: this appeared in the mid-1930s.

The Standard's format was changed, by the Kennel Club, in 1986. At the same time its wording was slightly altered, though none of the changes had any material effect on what earlier Standards had called for. The Kennel Club's revision to all Breed Standards entailed putting clauses in what the Kennel Club considered to be the order in

DECEMBER 14, 1923.

The Border Terrier Dog,
Champion
Grip of Tynedale

The property of
Messrs. Dodd & Carruthers,
"Oakwood," Hexham-on-Tyne

IT is forty-three years since Mr. J. Dodd first exhibited a Border Terrier. It was at Bellingham Show, and since then Mr. Dodd, who has won laurels as a Coursing, Greyhound, and Hound Trail judge, has never been without the breed, and is at the present time one of the most successful Border Terrier fanciers.

Messrs. Dodd and Carruthers have had a wonderful record this season with their small kennel, having won over one hundred prizes since last February. CH. GRIP OF TYNEDALE has won over sixty prizes, including four championships. He is one of the most typical Border Terriers living, for he possesses a grand " otter "-shaped head, splendid coat, and the best of legs and feet. Sired by the famous North Tyne Gyp, he belonged to a family of Border Terriers great in the annals of the show bench —viz., Ch. Themis, Ch. Tinker, Daphne, Dandy, Clincher, Allen Piper, Sambo, Bess, etc., and all are good game Terriers with a fox. His stock are most promising. His son, Jack of Tynedale, won the puppy class (10 entries) at the late Palace Kennel Club Show. Others sired by him are Cissy of Tynedale (recently

CH. GRIP OF TYNEDALE.

*Dodd and Caruthers'
advertisement in Our Dogs,
14 December 1923.*

which the attributes described are examined by judges. This implied that the Breed Standard's main purpose was as a guide for judges, and that all judges methodically examine each part of the dog in a strict sequence. In fact the use of Breed Standards by judges is incidental to their use as a guide for breeders whose order of priorities may be very different from the examination routine adopted by judges. The basic Standard requires amplification, interpretation and explanation before it is of real value to judges, especially those whose experience lies mainly in other breeds.

The Kennel Club's revision did, however, allow the introduction of one change for which the breed's supporters were grateful. At the end of the Standard are two clauses which appear in every Breed Standard: the first of these reads: 'Faults: Any departure from the foregoing points should be considered a fault, and the seriousness with which the fault should be regarded should be in exact proportion to its degree', – to which is added, in the Border Terrier Standard – 'and its effect on the terrier's ability to work'. This phrase not only rein-forced the importance of functional qualities, it also gave some guidance to the importance of various characteristics: thus more significance should be attached to faults which interfere with the ability to work than to those which have no such effect. Unfortunately the value of this change was reduced when subsequent influential Kennel Club publications omitted this very welcome addition to the Standard.

The final clause also appears in all breed standards, and reads as such: 'NOTE: Male animals should have two apparently normal testi-cles fully descended into the scrotum'. The purpose of this clause was to exert some influence over the incidence of a potentially serious hereditary defect, cryptorchidism, a defect which is far more seriously regarded in many overseas countries where dogs which are not entire can neither be shown nor bred from. Unfortunately in 1990 the Kennel Club went a long way towards making even this tentative clause obsolete when it decided to allow castrated dogs to be shown, and even to win their way into the Stud Book! These changes apart, the revised Kennel Club Breed Standard does not differ materially from that which it replaced, so for our purposes it can be ignored.

It is an interesting and salutary exercise to compare the six Breed Standards. To do so we will list the clauses as they appeared in the 1920 Border Terrier Club Breed Standard, which stressed that the points were listed in order of importance. This order is not without signifi-cance today. Thus the opening clause might be seen as an attempt to define type; this is followed by size, which in a terrier intended to work to fox is vitally important. Then comes the description of the head and its properties – not, perhaps, important to function, but the characteristic which most obviously establishes type. The body and legs are described next, and last of all the coat and colour. The order can be seen as one which relates closely to function, but it can also be viewed as one which places qualities which are unlikely to change above those which are subject to seasonal changes.

DECEMBER 8, 1922.

THE CELEBRATED
Kennel of Border Terriers,

The Property of Mr. & Mrs. Geo. Sordy, Titlington, Glanton, Northumberland.

CH. TITLINGTON TATLER.

Titlington Tatler, as illustrated in the 8 December 1922 issue of Our Dogs.

Since the first interest in Kennel Club recognition began to stir, the Border Terrier has had a number of Breed Standards, some official, some not. Prior to recognition in 1920 none of the Standards had any official status, but are no less interesting for that. After 1920 the Standard presumably written by Hamilton Adams was approved by the Kennel Club, but it was almost immediately scrapped in favour of the Border Terrier Club's own Standard. Since the 1920 Kennel Club Standard was not written by Border Terrier breeders and was never used, it now has little more than historic interest. The short-lived Northumberland Border Terrier Club produced its own Standard, and

37

some time in the 1930s, the Border Terrier Club produced a revised Standard which was accepted by the Kennel Club; with no more than minor modification, this one remained in use until 1988 when changes albeit of little material consequence, were imposed by the Kennel Club.

Pre-Recognition Breed Standards

1909 Jacob Robson	1913 *Illustrated Kennel News*	1915 Fred Morris
GENERAL	Gallant little dogs,. . . . game and sturdy sportsman, the foxhunter's friend, game, hard-bitten little Terrier, the hero of many a fight in craig and moss. Not unlike a small Irish Terrier.	Clean in his habits, very intelligent, affectionate game little terrier.
SIZE	From 14 to 16 lb.	About 14 inches at the shoulders and weighing about 14 or 15 pounds.
HEAD		
Their ears ought to hang like a Fox Terrier's but this is not a *sine qua non*. A strong jaw is a good point; not nearly so long in the nose as a Dandie or a Scottish Terrier. Either red or black nosed, but the red-nosed ones are often the keenest scented.	Rather short, but of good width. The ears are carried well back like those of a Foxhound. Jaws of tremendous power.	Skull moderately strong and not flat on top. Rather small, filbert shaped, dropping close to the head Very much shorter and stronger than that of a fox-terrier in jaw.
EYES	Dark, piercing.	Not too small, bright and keen.

1909	1913	1915
Jacob Robson	*Illustrated Kennel News*	**Fred Morris**

BODY

Have a short back, not made like a Dandie Dinnont, long backed and crooked.	Short, well-knit body. Shoulders should be narrow with straight front. Must not be too low to ground, as he frequently has to gallop many miles with the huntsman.	

FORELEGS

They should stand straight on their legs.		Straight

FEET

	Small and round.	Cat-like with good pads and toes closely knit together.

STERN

HINDQUARTERS

COAT

Hard, wiry, and close so as to enable them to withstand wet and cold.	Hard, wiry.	Wiry and weather resisting with the hair not too long and lying close to the body with a good undercoat. This class of coat is preferred for the moss or peat holes. Old fanciers perfer the dog free from topknot and do not care for the very broken coat.

COLOUR

The favourite colour is red or mustard, although plenty of the variety are pepper coloured and a few black-and-tan.	Rich reddish hue for preference, though blues, too, are frequently seen.	Red or grey-brindled, a dark blue body and tan legs. Livers are often found but red is the favourite colour, with dark muzzle and dark velvety ears.

Post-Recognition Breed Standards

The Breed Standard that the Kennel Club approved, after they agreed
to recognize Border Terriers in 1920, follows:

Weight about 14lb. Head otter-shaped, comparatively wide in skull;
short broad muzzle with even teeth; ears drop; eyes dark and small.
Body, medium length; deep ribs, well carried back, but not so sprung
as those of a Fox Terrier. Front straight and narrow. Forelegs straight
but with less bone than those of a Fox Terrier. Hindquarters galloping.
Coat dense, harsh, with good undercoat. Skin, thick, and red, wheaten
or grizzle. These dogs run with packs.

At the same time, the Border Terrier Club drew up its own standard.
They were followed by the Northumberland Border Terrier Club. In
the 1930s, these two standards were combined:

1920 Border Terrier Club	1921 Northumberland Border Terrier Club	1930s Border Terrier Club
GENERAL		
Essentially a working terrier and being of necessity able to follow a horse, must combine great activity with gameness.		The Border Terrier is essentially a working terrier and, it being necessary that it should be able to follow a horse, must combine activity with gameness.
SIZE		
Dogs should be between 14lb and 17lb in weight and 16 inches in height at shoulder. Bitches should not exceed 15lb in weight and 15 inches in height at shoulder	Dogs 14lb Bitches 13lb maximum	Dogs 13 to 15½lb. Bitches between 13½ and 14lb.

1920 Border Terrier Club	1921 Northumberland Border Terrier Club	1930s Border Terrier Club
HEAD Like that of an otter, moderately broad in skull. Short, strong muzzle. Level teeth Black nose preferred but liver- and flesh-coloured not to disqualify Small, V-drop ears	Otter shaped. The skull should be flat and wide. Jaws powerful and not pointed. Mouth, level: under shot or pig jaw no use. Nose, black or flesh coloured. Ears, small and curved rather to the side of the cheek.	Like that of an otter, moderately broad in skull. Short strong muzzle. Level teeth. A black nose is preferred, but a liver or flesh coloured one is not objectionable. Small V-shaped of moderate thickness and dropping forward close to the cheek.
EYES Dark with keen expression.		Dark with keen expression.
BODY Deep, narrow, and fairly long, ribs carried well back, but not over-sprung, as a terrier should be capable of being spanned by both hands behind the shoulder.	Neck, moderate length, slightly arched and sloping gracefully into the shoulder. Not too long and well ribbed up. Chest narrow. Shoulders long, sloping and set well back.	Deep and narrow and fairly long. ribs carried well back, but not oversprung, as a terrier should be capable of being spanned by both hands behind the shoulder. Loin strong.
FORELEGS Straight, not too heavy in bone.	True and muscular and not out at the elbow.	Straight and not too heavy in bone.
FEET Small and cat-like.		Small with thick pads.

1920	1921	1930s
Border Terrier Club	**Northumberland Border Terrier Club**	**Border Terrier Club**

STERN

Short, undocked, thick at base, then tapering set high, carried gaily, but not curled over the back.

Well carried and not curved over the back.

Moderately short and fairly thick at base then tapering, set high and carried gaily but not curled over the back.

HINDQUARTERS

Racing.

Racing.

COAT

Harsh and dense with close undercoat.

Wiry and hard with good undercoat.

Harsh and dense with close undercoat.

SKIN

Thick.
Colour red, wheaten, grizzle or blue and tan.

Thick.
Colour, red, wheaten, grizzle and tan, or blue and tan.

DISQUALIFICATIONS

Mouth undershot, or much overshot.

Points:

Head, ears neck and teeth	20
Legs and feet	15
Coat and skin	10
Shoulders and chest	10
Eyes and expression	10
Back and loin	10
Hindquarters	10
Tail	5
General appearance	10
TOTAL	100

The Modern Breed Standards

In 1988 agreement between the Kennel Club and the breed clubs resulted in a revised Breed Standard which would be used both in Britain and in those countries which owed allegiance to the Fédération Cynologique Internationale (FCI). The new standard contained few material changes from that which had served the breed so well since the 1930s, though its style was significantly different. In 1988 the Border Terrier Club of America, working with the American Kennel Club, also produced a revised Breed Standard. Comparison between the two exposes important similarities and a few differences.

UK Breed Standard (Reproduced by kind permission of the Kennel Club.)	**American Breed Standard** (Reproduced by kind permission of the American Kennel Club.)
	Since the Border Terrier is a working Terrier of a size to go to ground and able, within reason, to follow a horse, his conformation should be such that he be ideally built to do his job. No deviations from this ideal conformation should be permitted, which would impair his usefulness in running his quarry to earth and in bolting it therefrom. For this work he must be alert, active and agile, and capable of squeezing through narrow apertures and rapidly traversing any kind of terrain. His head like that of an otter," is distinctive, and his temperament ideally exemplifies that of a Terrier. . . . It should be the aim of Border Terrier breeders to avoid such over-emphasis of any point in the Standard as might lead to unbalanced exaggeration.
GENERAL APPEARANCE Essentially a working terrier.	He is an active Terrier of medium bone, strongly put together, suggesting endurance and agility, but rather narrow in shoulder, body and quarter. The body is covered with a somewhat broken though close-fitting and intensely wiry jacket. The

characteristic "otter" head with its keen eye, combined with body poise which is "at the alert," gives a look of fearless and implacable determination characteristic of the breed. The proportions should be that the height at the withers is slightly greater than the distance from the withers to the tail, i.e., by possibly 1–1½ inches in a 14 pound dog.

CHARACTERISTICS

Capable of following a horse, combining activity with gameness.

TEMPERAMENT

Active and game as previously stated.

By nature he is good-tempered, affectionate, obedient, and easily trained. In the field he is hard as nails, "game as they come" and driving in attack.

HEAD & SKULL

Head like that of an otter but moderately broad in skull.

Similar to that of an otter. Moderately broad and flat in skull with plenty of width between the eyes and between the ears. A slight, moderately broad curve at the stop rather than a pronounced identation. Cheeks slightly full.

MUZZLE

Short, strong muzzle.

Short and "well filled". A dark muzzle is characteristic and desirable. A few short whiskers are natural to the breed.

NOSE

Black nose preferable, but liver or flesh coloured one not a serious fault.

Black, and of good size.

EYES

Dark with keen expression.

Dark hazel and full of fire and intelligence. Moderate in size, neither prominent nor small and beady.

EARS

Small, V-shaped, of moderate thickness, and dropping forward close to the cheek.

Small, V-shaped and of moderate thickness, dark preferred. Not set high on the head but somewhat on the side, and dropping forward close to the cheeks. They should not break above the level of the skull.

MOUTH

Scissor bite, i.e. upper teeth closely overlapping lower teeth and set square to the jaws. Level bite acceptable. Undershot or overshot are major faults and highly undersirable.

TEETH

Strong, with a scissors bite, large in proportion to size of dog.

NECK

Of moderate length.

Clean, muscular and only long enough to give a well-balanced appearance. It should gradually widen into the shoulder.

SHOULDERS

Well laid back and of good length, the blades converging to the withers gradually from a brisket not excessively deep or narrow.

FOREQUARTERS

Forelegs straight, not too heavy in bone.

FORELEGS

Straight and not too heavy in bone and placed slightly wider than in a Fox Terrier.

BODY

Deep, narrow, fairly long. Ribs carried well back, but not oversprung, as a terrier should be capable of being spanned by both hands behind the shoulder. Loins strong.

Deep, fairly narrow and of sufficient length to avoid any suggestions of lack of range and agility. Deep ribs carried well back and not oversprung in view of the desired depth and narrowness of the body. The body should be capable of being spanned by a man's hands behind the shoulders. Back strong but laterally supple, with no suspicion of a dip behind the shoulder. Loin strong and the underline fairly straight.

FEET

Small with thick pads.

Small and compact. Toes should point forward and be moderately arched with thick pads.

TAIL

Moderately short; fairly thick at base, then tapering.

Moderately short, thick at the base, then tapering. Not set on too high. Carried gaily when at the alert, but not over the back. When at ease, a Border may drop his stern.

GAIT/MOVEMENT

Has the soundness to follow a horse.

Straight and rhythmical before and behind, with good length of stride and flexing of stifle and hock. The dog should respond to his handler with a gait which is free, agile and quick.

COAT

Harsh and dense; with close undercoat.

A short and dense undercoat covered with a very wiry and somewhat broken top coat which should lie closely, but it must not show any tendency to curl or wave. With such a coat a Border should be abler to be exhibited almost in his natural state, nothing more in the way of trimming being needed than a tidying-up of the head, neck and feet.

SKIN

Must be thick.

HIDE

Very thick and loose fitting.

COLOUR

Red, wheaten, grizzle and tan or blue and tan.

COLOR

Red, grizzle and tan, blue, or wheaten. A small amount of white may be allowed on the chest but white on the feet should be penalised.

SIZE

Dogs 5.9–7.1kg (13–15½lb). Bitches 5.1–6.4kg (11½–14lb).

Dogs. 13–15½ pounds, bitches 11½–14 pounds, are appropriate weights for Border Terriers in hard condition.

Head, ears, neck and teeth	20
Legs and feet	15
Coat and skin	10
Shoulders and chest	10
Eyes and expression	10
Back and loin	10
Hindquarters	10
Tail	5
General appearance	10
TOTAL	100

Frank Townend Barton, a veterinary surgeon, 'had a number of Border Terriers through his hands and has always been satisfied with the meritorious qualities most of these dogs possessed'; nevertheless he was far from sanguine about the prospects of the breed ever becoming popular. 'It is very questionable,' he wrote in his *Kennel Encyclopaedia*, 'whether these dogs will ever be popular, because it is a breed which has nothing remarkable about it in appearance; in fact, a novice in kennel classics might easily overlook any particular features characteristic of the Border terrier.'

The terrier volume of Rawdon Lee's *Modern Dogs* published in 1894 and claimed by the author to be the first book exclusively devoted to terriers – describes Border Terriers as,

. . . one of the most useful strains of terriers which still survives, and has done so without the bolstering up of any specialist clubs or dog shows, but lives and excels on its own merits alone, is a rough and ready sort of dog kept in Northumberland and on the Borders. This dog is neither a Dandie Dinmont nor a Bedlington Terrier, and I am inclined to agree with what those who keep it say, that it is an older breed than either . . . Lately the name 'Border Terrier' has been given to them, an apt enough nomenclature, but whether they require any particular designation now after doing their work so well for a hundred years, and perhaps more, is an open question.

Lee's attitude is puzzling in that he seems to suggest that the breed hadn't previously had a name, and having 'lately' been given one, didn't really need one.

Interpreting the Breed Standard

Breeders and exhibitors all over the world keep themselves amused and away from more serious mischief by engaging in endless discussion about what may be the most important characteristics of their respective breeds. Efforts are made to compile a hierarchy of faults and virtues. In the past it was common to ascribe points to different characteristics and by arriving at a total to arrive also at an assessment of the whole. In some countries and for some breeds a similar system remains in use and has doubtless progressed into the computer age so that it may not be long before machines and not people will be assessing dogs.

Fascinating though the arguments often are and reluctant though we are to forego the entertainment they provide, in our view they rely almost entirely on sheer sophistry. In reality there is no argument. Among the most important of the words in the old Breed Standard were the four with which it began: '**The Border Terrier is. . .** ', those four words emphasizing the fact that the Standard is about Border Terriers, and helping to stress the importance of breed type; also the next four words, '**essentially a working terrier**', effectively said what Border Terriers are for. There are other working terriers which are not Border Terriers, and other terriers which are neither working terriers nor Border Terriers; but there should never be any confusion or compromise in the Border Terrier between type and the qualities needed by a working terrier.

Borders, hounds and horses mix well.

The most important characteristic of any Border Terrier is that it should look like a Border Terrier. The Breed Standard, of course, stipulates that a Border Terrier is essentially a working terrier. The word 'essential' is applied to no other characteristic, and so it might be concluded that the most important trait of a Border Terrier is that it should be capable of doing the job for which the breed was brought into being. Without in any way denigrating the importance of functional qualities – indeed we will presently defend what we regard as their vital importance – it has to be accepted that there are other breeds of working terrier in Britain which do precisely the same job as Border Terriers, and which may do it equally well – indeed, their supporters may even suggest that they do it better! They are superb working terriers but they are not Border Terriers, leading us to the conclusion that a terrier can be a good working terrier without being a Border Terrier. Thus type, the sum of all those qualities which differentiate Border Terriers from all other breeds, must be paramount.

Soundness, physical as well as temperamental, is another important quality which few would disagree might also, with complete justification, be described as essential, both to the breed's ability to perform the tasks expected of a working terrier, and in the show ring and the home – or it should be.

The Standard continues by saying, for reasons which should now be obvious, that '**It should be able to follow a horse and must combine activity with gameness**'. Cardboard cut-outs may look pretty in the ring but fail to suggest the necessary degree of activity; and it must once more be stressed that '**gameness**' might not be found in a quarrelsome or indiscriminately aggressive terrier, because such a terrier is likely to be cowardly when faced with a real opponent; in which case it would certainly be useless for the sort of life a working terrier must lead.

The Standard might appear to say nothing about movement, but this is because it assumes that those who read it will have a modicum of sense: thus a terrier which must be able to follow a horse and stay with hounds must be able to move with drive, economy and speed. Whilst on this point, judges should be careful not to confuse flashiness with drive, or exuberance with unsoundness. Nor does the Standard appear to give much guidance about temperament, although judges who know what the breed is for and who appreciate the demands made on a working terrier will need no such guidance; once more, the Standard's original authors gave their readers credit for some intelligence.

'**Head like that of an otter, moderately broad in skull, with a short strong muzzle**'. There is something almost reptilian about the basic lines of an otter's head, the muzzle being broad, short and powerful, and not made to look so by carefully sculpted hair: the line from the nose, over the smoothly contoured stop, across the skull and down the strong but elegant neck is a series of smooth curves. And regarding the features, judges in Britain are unlikely to see noses which are *not* black, although they might see eyes which are not '**dark, with keen expression**'. The colour of the eyes and of the coat, and the required length of the tail are the only three clauses in the Standard in which its original authors allowed themselves the luxury of departing from matters which had a direct bearing on function. Perhaps for this reason they are matters which seem sometimes to have regrettably low priority.

Ears should be '**small, V-shaped, of moderate thickness and dropping forward close to the cheek**'. A thin ear would be easily damaged; a thick, fleshy one would, if damaged, take a long time to heal; and a flap which did not protect the inner ear would be of little use. Heavy, hound-like ears, traditionally described as being like a 'cobbler's apron', are neither attractive nor useful.

Jack Price's homebred Ch. Oxcroft Rocker.

'**Teeth should have a scissor-like grip, with the top teeth slightly in front of the lower, but a level mouth is quite acceptable. An undershot or overshot mouth is a major fault and highly undesirable**'. It takes little thought to realize that a toothless terrier would be at some disadvantage when facing a fox – and it therefore requires but little more to appreciate that a full complement of big, strong, evenly spaced teeth would be of great value. Terriers with faulty dentition can and do work, but their working lives are shortened as teeth are rapidly lost.

The Standard produced by the short-lived Northumberland Border Terrier Club contained the unequivocal statement 'pig-jawed no use'. 'Pig-jawed' referred to an overshot mouth, technically a brachygnathic mouth – one in which the incisors in the upper jaw protruded in front of those in the lower jaw. Other Standards have been less forthright, but wise breeders, exhibitors and judges tend to share the Northumberland Club's view. Nor are they alone. 'Never breed from a "Swine chopped" hound – it is also very hereditary', said the Earl of Lonsdale in *Foxhunting*. Daphne Moore's *The Book of the Foxhound* is equally forthright: 'Ideally, should such a mouth be discovered among a litter of whelps they should all be put down and a note made of the line to be avoided. . . . It is extremely important for the future of Foxhound Breeding that swine chops should not be perpetuated, and no hound with this defect, however good in its work, should be bred from.' What in this respect is right for the Foxhound, is also right for the Border Terrier.

Perhaps as a consequence of virtually unanimous condemnation, overshot mouths are seldom seen in the breed. Undershot mouths are a different matter, however, and although equally objectionable they appear to be more readily tolerated. Indeed there have been champions which have been undershot. Unless undershot mouths are condemned as heartily as are overshot mouths, the problem – an inherited condition – will become progressively more troublesome.

'**Neck of moderate length**': length of neck is, of course, a product of shoulder construction, and well laid shoulders will produce a neck which is neither stuffy nor swan-like. Forelegs should be '**straight and not too heavy in bone**', since fine bone would not withstand the stress of a day on the fells, whilst heavy bone would be an unnecessary encumbrance; like so many other places in the Standard, the touchstone is 'moderation'. Obviously a fair length of leg is required in order to give the necessary agility and ability to cover the ground.

*Jean and Frank Jackson's Ch.
Clipstone Cetchup. (Photo.
William Moores.)*

A '**deep and narrow and fairly long**' body provides the necessary heart and lung room to fuel stamina without the sort of excessive width or depth which would impede the terrier underground. It must be remembered that legs can be bent to squeeze into a narrow hole (who ever saw a short-legged fox?), but ribs are much less flexible, and that is why the Standard says they should be '**not over-sprung**' and suggests that '**a terrier should be capable of being spanned by both hands behind the shoulder**'. Of course, this clause was originally written long before it was thought possible that ladies, some of whom might have ladylike hands, would ever judge the breed. Spanning a terrier and – as most judges do – lifting it off the table, not only provides a judge with information about ribs, but also about overall balance, the way the dog 'comes to hand', and about temperament. It also demonstrates to exhibitors that the judge has at least read the Standard.

The loin should be '**strong**', and since the body should be '**fairly long**' it follows that it should not be closely coupled. A strong loin is necessary to any dog which must cover considerable distances during the course of a day's work, while a reasonable length gives the flexibility to manoeuvre underground. Compare the ease with which a Border can put its nose on its tail with the difficulty experienced by short-backed, short-coupled breeds, and you will get some idea of the importance of fair length of back and a good, strong coupling. A short-backed Border might look smart, but it doesn't look right to the discerning eye and it would be at a disadvantage underground.

Jean Jackson's and Carl Gunnar Stafberg's Int. Ch. Bombax Xavier. (Photo. SEM.)

No breed other that the Border Terrier has a Standard which uses a single word, '**racy**', to describe the hindquarters. Nor has it ever been thought necessary to augment that one word because, taken with the rest of the Standard, it says it all: a Border Terrier is neither a cart-horse which needs an exaggerated bend of stifle, nor a sprinter which needs a high hock to impart the leverage from which speed develops. It is a dog which will be expected to canter all day across rough country, and '**racy**' says all.

'**Small feet with thick pads**' are an obvious necessity for any breed intended to work in rough country; thin, open feet are prone to damage.

The tail – and Border Terrier breeders are expected to have sufficient skill to breed dogs with naturally short tails – is an appendage on which the Standard's original authors tended to concentrate all their aesthetic feelings. Old breeders used to wax lyrical over comparisons with the tines of harrows or with obscure varieties of carrot. It is to be expected that a 'gay stern' would be abominated by anyone who knows about Foxhounds. A tail which is '**moderately short and fairly thick at the base, then tapering, set high and carried gaily**' 'finishes off' the dog without calling for any unacceptable exaggerations.

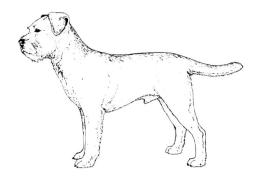

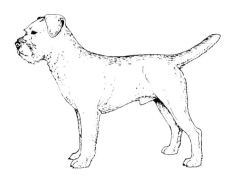

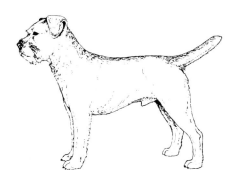

Left above: Basic outline
Left centre: Over deep
Left below: Gay Stern
Centre above: Short back
Centre: Overangulation
Centre below: Short legs
Right above: Pump Handle Tail
Right centre: Weak loin
Right below: Upright in front

Coats – or rather pelts, because the skin must be included – are another matter. A good, hard, close, weather-resistant top coat with a dense undercoat and a thick skin to provide protection as well as insulation should need no justification; their importance to a working terrier is often a matter of life and death. In the show ring, clever presentation may offer a superficially smarter appearance, though more often recourse to scissors is obvious and the result ugly; but what use would be a well cut silk dress to someone who is expected to spend a winter's day on the fells of Northumberland? However, judges should be careful not to confuse a skin underlain with fat with a genuine thick pelt. In terms of work it might, reasonably, be argued that, like horses, a good Border can't be a bad colour. There is, however, some prejudice in the hunting field against terriers which resemble a fox in colour, because it is suggested that hounds might mistake one for the other. What certainly might happen is that what Beckford described as **'awkward people'** might make such a mistake, but in our experience (which is now longer than is comfortable), hounds are far more discerning than are 'awkward people'.

The November 1991 issue of the *Kennel Gazette* contained an announcement which was not without significance to all Border Terrier breeders, and had considerable import for many:

Registrations – Colour of Dogs

In the registration of Pedigree dogs it is Kennel Club policy to record the actual colour of the animal. Where this is incompatible with colours permitted in the Breed Standard, the colour will be endorsed 'non Standard'.

All breeders, exhibitors and judges were aware that the only colours mentioned in the Standard were red, wheaten, grizzle and tan, and blue and tan. It seemed that, in future, these would be the only colours which would be allowed to appear on Kennel Club Border Terrier registration documents without being accompanied by the sinister-sounding phrase 'non-Standard'. Apparently the Kennel Club had taken this step in order to prevent breeders, in some breeds other than Borders, from deliberately, or by chance, producing dogs of unusual and unacceptable colours and then marketing them as rare and valuable specimens of their breed. As far as we are aware the problem didn't exist in Borders, so, far from solving problems, the change actually *created* them for Border Terrier breeders.

Some of the old breeders seem to have disregarded the Standard as far as colour is concerned when they registered their puppies. For example Coquetdale Reward, Fearsome Fellow, Furious Fighter and Miss Tut were all described as brindle by Adam Forster. Sir John Renwick registered Newminster Radiant as black and tan, Newminster Rummy was a blue grizzle, Phyllis Mulcaster registered Portholme Mab as red with black mask, and Portholme Jan was wheaten with black mask.

Among the old champions there was red wheaten Ch. Hasty Light, dark red Ch. Ivo Roisterer, slightly grizzled Ch. Jedworth Bunty, brindle Ch. Ranter, tan, dark ears and muzzle Ch. Rona Rye, red grizzle Ch. Foxlair, red and grizzle Ch. Deerstone Driver, dark grizzle Ch. Cherisette, golden Ch. Golden Sovereign.

It is necessary only to look back through old registrations to realize that the colours of a significant number of Border Terriers have been described in ways in which do not conform with the Breed Standard. Black and tan, blue grizzle, bright red, brindle, brown, dark grizzle, dark grizzle and tan, dark red, fawn, fawn grizzle, golden, grizzle, grizzle wheaten, grizzle with dark back, light brown, light grizzle, liver, mustard, red and grizzle, red grizzle, red slightly grizzled, red wheaten, red with black mask, red with black muzzle, red with dark sides, sandy, tan with dark ears and muzzle, tan with dark sides, wheaten with black mask are among the many non-Standard descriptions which have been used in the past, with red grizzle and dark grizzle appearing by far the most frequently.

We are quite certain that none of these terms was used with any intention to deceive. What the majority of breeders were probably trying to do was to provide a more accurate description of their puppies than strict conformity with the Breed Standard would allow. Even so, the Kennel Club's edict appeared to mean that if these or similar helpful descriptions were to be used, they would be qualified as 'non-Standard'.

All of which put Border Terrier breeders in a dilemma. Unless the Kennel Club could be persuaded to accept the continued use of some colour descriptions which don't appear in the Breed Standard, red grizzle, dark and possibly light grizzle perhaps being the most obvious ones, breeders would be obliged to choose between three courses, all of which had attendant problems. By continuing to use non-Standard terms in an effort to describe colours more accurately, the problem loomed large of providing buyers with what they would regard as an acceptable explanation when the words 'non Standard' appeared on registration documents. If descriptions were confined to the four colours which appear in the Breed Standard, accuracy would be sacrificed and future breeders would be denied the benefit of the sort of information former breeders have thoughtfully provided. The third course would have been to consider changes to the Standard so that colours could be accurately described without the words 'non Standard' appearing on registration documents.

But there was another problem associated with colour, one which would have to be resolved before new colours were introduced into the Breed Standard. Indeed, even if nothing were changed, breeders would find it helpful to have the problem resolved. The Standard offered the choice of red, wheaten, grizzle and tan, and blue and tan. What it didn't do was provide a precise definition of what these four terms mean, and it seemed that, in an Alice-in-Wonderlandish sort of way, they could mean almost anything breeders wanted them to mean. Obviously such a situation, even though it had been with us since 1920, was far from satisfactory.

Weight is too often confused with size: thus, a ribby terrier on stumpy legs might weigh 12lb (5.5kg) and be far too big to be useful. A narrow, leggy creature might weigh 17lb (7.6kg) or even 18lb (8kg) and yet be able to follow almost any fox. What is needed is a range, such as the Standard calls for, which will furnish the breed with terriers capable of doing any job. After all, foxes do not come in standard sizes and neither do the places in which they might take refuge. A small bitch of about 12lb will be able to get into places which might be inaccessible for a larger, 15½lb (6.7kg) dog which, faced with high or wide obstacles underground or the need to support persuasion with a little muscle, would then come into his own. If the breed is to retain its complete value as a working terrier it needs all the range of size allowed by the Standard. Judges who look for uniformity of size expose their lack of knowledge of what the breed is for, and those who do not know what the breed is for should not be judging it.

During the late 1980s the Waltham Centre for Animal Nutrition, as part of the service which Pedigree Petfoods provide for breeders and exhibitors, provided the facilities at major British Championship Shows for dogs to be accurately weighed. The information gleaned as a result of this service must be treated with caution, since it relied entirely on dogs whose owners regarded them as of a quality suitable for competition at Championship Shows, and since only a relatively small number of Border Terriers were examined; but it is, nevertheless, both interesting and revealing.

The Breed Standard requires that adult dogs should weigh between

13 and 15.5lb (5.9 and 7.1kg) and adult bitches between 11.5 and 14lb (5.1 and 6.4kg). The mean weight for dogs would be 14.25lb (6.5kg) and for bitches 12.75lb (5.75kg). The survey revealed that the mean weight for dogs was 17.68lb (8.04kg) within a range 14.3–21.56lb (6.6–9.8kg). The mean weight for bitches was 15.33lb (6.97kg) within a range from 12.76–18.04 lb(5.8–8.2kg).

The evidence suggests that Border Terriers shown at major British Championship Shows during the late 1980s tended to be heavier, and in some cases far heavier, than the Standard regards as desirable. What we don't know, because the survey preserves the anonymity of individual dogs and bitches, is whether the terriers which were far heavier than the Standard recommends achieved significant success in the ring.

Perhaps the results of the survey can be used to give cautious support to a feeling that Border Terriers, in common with the majority of breeds, have been tending to become heavier over the years. It would not be surprising if improved standards of care, better nutrition, freedom from parasites and, possibly, less exercise resulted in dogs being heavier than they were when the breed first achieved recognition. Whether this increase in weight is in the breed's best interests is debatable. What is certain is that, if the breed is to retain any pretensions to being a genuine working terrier, the trend must be halted before the breed becomes too heavy to do the job for which it is intended.

4

The New Puppy

Every year, well over half a million British people buy a puppy. A large number have never previously owned a dog and have only a hazy idea about what they should look for; equally, many have never had charge of any animal and may not realize what is involved regarding its daily care thoughout its life. If they were to rely on the experience of making other purchases they might be inclined to believe that their best course would be to buy from a kennel which advertises widely and can offer a choice of several breeds. However, nothing could be further from the truth.

The first question which must be asked is whether you really do want a puppy at all: perhaps a pet of another species would better suit your needs? Prospective purchasers are often advised to look for a breed which will suit their lifestyle. In fact, introducing a puppy into a home which did not previously contain a dog will bring inevitable changes – indeed, the main purpose of buying a puppy may be to promote change. Dog ownership offers companionship, and it may be an encouragement to take exercise, or a means to improve health; it may also be a way of making friends, a means of security or a way to take part in competitions, a source of pride and interest – but it brings with it the absolute responsibility of ensuring that the dog is well cared for and does not cause nuisance or danger to others. Well cared for dogs do not wander the streets, nor do they produce unwanted puppies or foul public places; they are not uncontrollably noisy, but are obedient, clean and a source of joy and pride to their owners.

Every dog owner and most prospective owners will have selected a breed which totally captivates them. This besotted devotion may be based on nothing more than irrational romanticism or sheer nostalgia – but it is a far firmer base for selecting a breed than are the coldly analytical processes intended to ensure that the chosen breed meets a certain set of computer-defined criteria much as would be employed in buying a domestic appliance or a used car. Choose a breed that you like, but do so in full knowledge of what ownership of that particular breed entails.

The best people to buy a puppy from are not usually those who need to market their puppies, but those who, one way and another, do not make it easy for potential purchasers. Always buy from a breeder, never from a dealer. It may not be easy, but buying from a breeder who reluctantly sells puppies which are the by-product of a breeding programme intended to produce outstandingly good dogs for use in competitions will certainly increase your chances of acquiring a healthy, well adjusted puppy. Puppies which are produced primarily for sale and marketed, whether by the breeder or less directly through a catalogue agency, may be less satisfactory than those bred by breeders whose primary aim is to produce puppies of outstanding quality but who are obliged to part with the ones they do not need themselves.

It is usually best to avoid puppies which are advertised as just another commodity available for sale or exchange. Certain adverts in the canine press will indicate a source where puppies have obviously enjoyed the benefit of a more concerned environment. Even here, however, it may be best to avoid those breeders who advertise several breeds, or seem to have a constant supply of puppies available. Puppies, and especially Border Terrier puppies, need individual care if they are to become satisfactorily socialized. Rearing one litter is a demanding and time-consuming operation; trying to rear several may mean that methods more appropriate to farm livestock have to be employed.

If the appeal of a breed is strong you will have learned a great deal about it long before you decide to become an owner. You will have read books and magazines, you will have visited shows and other events where fellow devotees of the breed gather to share their enthusiasm. If you have omitted this essential part of your education, time taken to repair the omission will be well spent. You will learn more about the breed, its peculiarities, its potential problems and its initial and ongoing costs, and you will meet other owners. Among these will be breeders, some of whom will have developed the ability to recognize a potential customer at one hundred yards in a thick fog. *Caveat emptor*: let the buyer beware. Be very wary of those who just happen to have the very best puppy they have ever bred which, in a spirit of saintly benefaction, they are willing to let you have. Beware of breeders bearing gifts!

It is not difficult to define the basic, unavoidable criteria to which any breeder regarded as responsible must comply. Thus, all breeding stock must be physically and temperamentally sound, healthy and typical of the breed. All breeding stock must be kept, and the puppies reared, in conditions which offer security, comfort, cleanliness, adequate nutritious and wholesome food, and where they can take sufficient exercise and gain experience. All puppies should be treated for parasite infestation using veterinary approved products. Moreover, every puppy must undergo a carefully planned socialization process designed to ensure that it will adapt well to new experiences, a new home and new owners. Puppies with suspect temperaments should never be offered for sale.

All matings must be carefully planned so as to minimize the chance that puppies will suffer from inherited defects. Matings which have produced diseased or defective puppies should *not* be repeated. No puppy should leave its original home until it is more than eight weeks old and unless it is in good health. Breeders who sell to countries which do not have effective animal protection legislation will not be regarded as responsible. Responsible breeders will only sell after a personal interview with the purchaser. All sales will be unconditional.

Perhaps the best way to identify a good breeder is through the personal recommendation of satisfied puppy purchasers. Use your own common sense to discover which breeders command general respect among their fellows. The aim of the best breeders is to produce puppies of outstanding quality. Not all will be of the same quality, of course, but the worst from a good breeder is likely to be very much better than the best from a poor breeder. Good breeders never operate on the hope that quantity will, by luck and good fortune, produce occasional quality. They plan their few litters with great care in an effort to produce the best possible puppies. They are unlikely to have a puppy immediately available and may already have a waiting list.

If this proves to be the case, try other top quality breeders – but do not let impatience tempt you to lower your standards: only the best is good enough.

Acquiring Your Dog

No-one should ever acquire a dog of any sort if they cannot reasonably expect, or do not intend to give it a good home for its whole life. Every owner should provide a dog with good living conditions, a good diet, adequate, regular exercise and health care. It should be trained and supervised to ensure that it is happy, and does not become a nuisance to others. All caring breeders will expect to be assured that these conditions will be met before they agree to part with a puppy: the vendor's concern is, or should be, entirely for the future welfare of the terrier which is being sold. The buyer will share this concern, but will also want to ensure that the dog is likely to satisfy his requirements. It is therefore essential that these requirements are identified at the outset.

Perhaps the most crucial selection that anyone will make in respect of Border Terriers is when they acquire their first one, because they will have to make a decision when they are least able to exercise all the processes which, with a modicum of good luck, will lead to a wise choice. In such circumstances the watchword should be 'care'. Thus it is with a degree of circumspection that a buyer should accept a proud breeder's estimate of the quality and virtues of a particular puppy. Some breeders regard all their ugly ducklings as swans, not because they intend to deceive, but simply out of an excess of uncritical and perhaps misplaced pride. It is not uncommon for dogs with serious and obvious faults to be sold as potential show dogs, or for breeders whose success in the ring has been less than meteoric to sell every puppy out of a litter as such, too. We have even known puppies to be sold with a guarantee that they would become champions by breeders who themselves had never owned, let alone bred a champion.

The story of the man who was persuaded that a mediocre puppy would mature into a top-quality show dog comes to mind. The hopes and expectations he had for the dog were quickly dashed as, with predictable persistence, it remained a very ugly duckling. He decided to let the breeder know of his disappointment:

'You know that dog I bought from you? Well, it's for sale.'

'Yes, it was when I had it.'

So, you may have to wait for your pup interminably, or so it may seem; but this period will enable you to confirm your enthusiasm for the breed, as well as to increase your knowledge of it, and eventually the time will come when you are invited to examine a litter which may contain a puppy meant for you.

Try to keep your excitement and emotions under control because you are reaching the point of greatest risk: you may be about to part with a considerable amount of money, to undertake demanding commitments and responsibilities, and to join the privileged and besotted clan whose lives are irretrievably changed but enormously enriched by owning a Border Terrier.

By now you will know something about the breeder: for example, that he or she has a good reputation, has produced top-quality puppies and is to be trusted. Even so, caution remains the watchword. You are not buying a disposable object but a creature which will depend on you for its very life.

If the breeder is unusually accommodating or has, perhaps inadvertently, divulged the fact that a litter is imminent, you may know, to the very day, when they are born. By all means inquire as to their number and sex but until they have their eyes open and are toddling about do not expect to be invited to inspect them. At this stage any careful breeder is anxious for the puppies' welfare and that alone, and your impatience or eagerness will hardly register on his or her list of priorities.

Rescue Dogs

As yet the breed is not one which suffers from the problems usually associated with heavily commercialized breeds. Most breeders are prepared either to take back dogs of their breeding or to help with re-homing them, providing, of course, the owner is not simply trying to evade the responsibilities which every dog owner must accept.

Occasionally Borders fall on hard times through no fault of their own: the death of their owner, a change in family circumstances or for some equally unpredictable reason. Such dogs usually transfer to new homes without difficulty, although even the most plausible and heart-rending story should be treated with caution until it is known to be true.

Rescue dogs, like ladies, may be slightly older than their stated age! Puppies or even young dogs very rarely need to be rescued.

Making a Choice

When you first visit the breeder, regard the visit as in part an inspection, and in part an opportunity for the breeder to examine *you*. Ensure that the puppies and their dam are well fed, well housed, clean and healthy. They should not be locked away in some dark, isolated kennel where they have no opportunity to learn about the outside world or to accumulate new experiences, both of which are essential to their future attitude to life.

Don't be surprised if the proud mum resents your attention to her pups, but be very circumspect if she does so to the point of becoming

A bed full of promises.

aggressive because she may well have passed down that tendency to the puppies and it could manifest itself in *their* character under less provocative circumstances. Of course, the dam will not be looking at her best; some bitches will shed virtually all their coat while rearing their puppies, and others will become almost skeletal in spite of a prodigious intake of food. Make some allowances – but having done so, remember that the puppies will have inherited half of their characteristics, good and bad, from their mother.

The puppies should all be clean, inquisitive, bright eyed and – metaphorically speaking – bushy tailed. Not all will react to your attentions in the same way. Given the opportunity, the more independent ones will prefer to go exploring, and most will be more interested in their breeder than in strangers. Remember that they live in a small but intensely competitive society in which each must take notice of the status and power of its siblings. These are not machines, but small beings with no more than a few weeks' experience of life. Even so, harden your heart against any puppy which is unusually small or which does not welcome human contact. And if any of the puppies seem off colour you would be wise to look elsewhere; infection can spread very quickly through an entire litter.

If all seems well, examine the dogs which remain on your shortlist to ensure as far as is possible that they do not have any obvious faults. Watch them run and play, and examine carefully those which catch your eye.

Hereditary Defects

Border Terriers remain remarkably free from hereditary defects, and those which do occur tend to be relatively uncommon and do not threaten the well-being of affected dogs. However, it must be remembered that no species, domestic or wild, is, or can ever be, totally free from defects which may be passed from one generation to another. About three thousand inherited defects exist in our own species, and about three hundred in domestic dogs.

Inherited defects are spread most quickly through a breed by those who ignore their existence and who persist in inbreeding to affected animals. If Border Terrier breeders are honest with themselves about any inherited defects which may appear, and as long as they avoid close inbreeding –except, perhaps, to animals of outstanding quality –there is no reason why the breed should not retain its robust health and soundness. It will then still be the case that the three hundred or so inherited diseases identified in domestic dogs are less likely to appear in Border Terriers than are the three thousand identified in man to be found in their owners.

Monorchids and Cryptorchids

In the past, unwise use of monorchid or unilateral cryptorchid stud-dogs, and of stud-dogs which produced a preponderance of monorchid or unilateral cryptorchid puppies, has led to this fault being far too prevalent in the breed. A unilateral cryptorchid, popularly referred to as a monorchid, has only one testicle descended into the scrotum. The dog will be fertile but will transmit the problem to its offspring. A bilateral cryptorchid has neither testicle descended into the scotum and is infertile. The conditions appear to have a complex and as yet, not fully understood form of inheritance; for example, there is some evidence that bitches which carry the genes have themselves a reduced level of fertility. Undescended testicles are more likely to develop tumorous growths. Male puppies should, at birth, have two testicles fully descended into the scrotum. Puppies which are abnormally developed should be avoided, and no dog which is in any way abnormally developed should ever be used at stud.

Every Kennel Club Breed Standard contains a clause which insists that 'Male animals should have two apparently normal testicles fully descended into the scrotum.' 'Apparently normal' should be taken to mean 'of the same size'. 'Fully descended' should, in Border Terriers, be taken to mean lying side by side, and not in tandem, in the scrotum. However, in spite of this clause the Kennel Club allows dogs which are not entire to be shown and bred from. Many other kennel clubs take a stricter and, in our view, more responsible attitude by banning such dogs from shows and refusing to register their progeny.

Undershot and Overshot Jaws

Jaw and teeth defects have always apparently been a problem in the Border Terrier, and unfortunately some breeders, and occasionally very successful ones, choose to ignore or *even* excuse it; there have been *champions* in Britain whose dentition was at odds with what the Breed Standard has always required. In fact, until a puppy has produced its adult teeth there can be no certainty that its adult mouth will be without faults.

The milk teeth in a puppy's upper jaw should evenly overlap those in the lower jaw, though not to such an excessive degree as might raise fears that the adult mouth will be overshot, that is with the teeth in the upper jaw protruding well in front of those in the lower jaw. As the old Northumberland Standard so succinctly put it, 'pig jaw no use'.

A more common fault is for the teeth of the lower jaw to protrude in front of those in the upper to produce an undershot mouth. This may be the consequence of the lower jaw's tendency to continue to develop after the upper jaw has stabilized. It may also be caused by the order in which adult teeth erupt, or by large teeth in a narrow jaw or, it is sometimes claimed, by allowing a puppy in play to stress a malleable lower jaw and teeth.

Border Terriers with imperfect mouths seldom prosper in the show ring, and should not be bred from.

Kinked Tails

It is difficult to know what importance should be attached to a kinked tail, but since the tail is an extension of the spine is seems no more than prudent to err on the side of caution. A tail may be damaged before, during or soon after birth, although the defect is, to all practical considerations, indistinguishable from one which is an inherited defect. The mode of inheritance is uncertain, and the best that can be said is that the tendency to produce kinked tails is familial.

White Patches

White coat on a Border Terrier is acceptable as a small patch on the chest, but even then it is not to be encouraged; to the purist's eye, any white is seen as a disfigurement. However, puppies are often born with some white hairs on the feet which tend to disappear within a few weeks. A white foot or leg is a different matter. Thirty years ago these were commonplace, and there has even been a champion which had white feet. However, it is some years since *we* saw a white-footed puppy, and we would nowadays be suspicious as to the authenticity of the pedigree of any Border Terrier puppy with white feet or legs.

Discussing Terms

Make your choice, and if you haven't already been interrogated, prepare yourself for this experience: the breeder will want to know exactly how you propose to care for your puppy. Are you, or someone, at home throughout the day to care for its needs? What other pets do you have? Are unruly children likely to threaten its well-being? You will face a host of questions, and woe betide you if each is not answered with total honesty. However, remember that any caring breeder is interested, first and foremost, in the puppy's welfare, and your needs come a poor second – and if it were otherwise you would be wise to seek a more responsible breeder.

Eventually you will make a choice, subject to the breeder's approval, and will be in a position to discuss terms. Prices vary from breeder to breeder, from puppy to puppy and from area to area, and the most expensive is not necessarily the best nor the cheapest the worst. You must rely on your own judgement – but never, ever be tempted into any arrangements, deferred terms, breeding terms, stud rights, partnerships or anything else which denies you total and unconditional ownership of your purchase.

Documentation

Then comes the paperwork. You will receive a pedigree: four generations is usual, although some breeders provide five and others only three. The important thing is that the pedigree is accurate, since deliberately to provide false information is an offence. You will receive a receipt, and in the majority of cases, registration documents. If these are not immediately available the receipt, or a separate document, must record that fact and undertake that they will be provided within a reasonable period. Make absolutely sure that registration means registration with the Kennel Club. There are a number of spurious organizations which run virtually worthless registration systems: any puppy registered with any of these should be regarded as unregistered, and the price should reflect this fact.

A puppy or adult which is not registered and cannot be so, will usually be appreciably cheaper than one which is. If you are buying a puppy with the intention of breeding or becoming involved in a Kennel Club regulated activity it is essential that it *is* registered, and that the registration does not include endorsements which might thwart your intentions.

The Kennel Club offers a number of endorsements which can prevent a puppy from having its name changed, producing registered progeny, from competing in any competitions held under Kennel Club rules, and from being eligible for an export pedigree. Purchasers should be aware of any such restrictions and the price asked should reflect their effect on the puppy's potential value.

Check that the registration documents describe the puppy accurately: the date of birth and sex must be correct, as must the colour. Any colour description which does not appear in the Breed Standard should be regarded as detracting from the puppy's value.

If the puppy has received any veterinary treatment prior to your purchase you should be informed, and details of the treatment provided in writing. Minor surgery which has incidental cosmetic effect may well result in the puppy being barred from Kennel Club shows, and prior veterinary treatment, especially if it has involved an insurance claim, may make it difficult to insure the puppy in the future. This does not, of course, include vaccination by a veterinarian.

Vaccination

Puppies usually receive their first of two protective injections at eight or ten weeks of age. Some breeders may delay the first until the puppies are twelve weeks old, by which time the majority will be ready for their second injection. If the puppy has been vaccinated you will receive a certificate which provides full details, including the name and address of the veterinarian who did the vaccination. Vaccination carried out by anyone other than a vet should be disregarded.

Home Comforts

Eventually you will reach the point at which you can take your puppy home. Spare a thought – indeed, several thoughts – for the puppy. Probably for the first time in its life it will be leaving the home in which it was born, leaving its dam and its siblings to face a totally unfamiliar world with people who may not be confident of their ability to care for such a small and vulnerable creature. How any puppy ever adjusts to such a terrifying situation is a mystery and a wonder!

Yet after just a brief period of adjustment, puppies of no more than a few weeks old which have only recently been parted from their

Relaxing on the show bench.

mother and perhaps never before been parted from their siblings, appear not only to accept their new life, but even to make adjustments intended to make it more to their liking!

Mum and pups.
(Photo. J. Jackson.)

Even so, introducing a puppy or an older individual into a new home requires for a degree of planning and preparation. Before the newcomer joins the household, a wise new owner will have taken steps to ensure that it has a secure enclosure, whether all or part of the garden, in which to take the air. And if it is to live out of doors, he will have erected a suitable kennel – indeed, sometime earlier in order that fumes from anything used in its construction will have had the chance to dissipate. If the puppy is to live in the house a suitable bed will have been provided, and placed where it can enjoy both security and privacy.

Bedding, a collar and lead, and a supply of food, preferably of the type to which the newcomer is accustomed, will all have been purchased. A dish to eat from and a water bowl – too heavy to be over-turned in play, or of a design which makes it difficult to overturn – will also be needed. Moreover the wise owner will have taken steps to guard against inevitable 'accidents' by laying in a supply both of kitchen rolls and of those excellent bacteriological sprays which almost miraculously neutralize offensive smells without replacing them with something equally offensive!

Membership of a breed club is well worthwhile. All the clubs run a number of shows, matches or rallies each year, and some stage other events aimed at education and enjoyment. Most also publish club yearbooks and newsletters which keep owners in touch with what is happening in the breed.

There is no hard and fixed rule about the age at which it is best to transfer a puppy to its new home. Obviously it cannot go before it is weaned, but once it is fully independent in many respects the sooner the transfer is made the better. Breeders tend to take a pragmatic attitude: thus if the puppy is going to a home where the owners are experienced in caring for young puppies, the transfer may be made at eight weeks. But if there is no prior experience, and particularly if the household contains children too young to understand a puppy's needs, the transfer may be delayed for a few further weeks.

There's a biscuit in there!

Breeders will often avoid parting with puppies just before Christmas; indeed, most try to avoid having pups at this time of year when conflicting activities are likely to assume importance.

If a puppy goes to its new home early in the day, it and its new family will have time to become acquainted and the puppy will have the opportunity to become familiar with its new surroundings before the time comes for it to face a night spent, perhaps for the first time in its life, without the company of siblings. This first lonely night can be made less stressful if the puppy has the company of something familiar, a piece of bedding perhaps.

Negotiating the see-saw.

Bedding

Puppies should be provided with a bed which even their most determined efforts cannot harm, or with one which is easily and cheaply replaced; a cardboard box, or rather a succession of cardboard boxes, is ideal.

House-Training

Puppies which have been reared in the house will already be some way along the road to being house-trained – though it has to be stressed that the move to a new home may lead to a temporary regression. Very young puppies may be trained to use newspaper, or one of the absorbent pads manufactured for the purpose. As soon as they are old enough to venture outside or into an indoor run, that is where they should be fed. They should then be allowed time to empty themselves, and should be praised lavishly when they have done so.

The key to house-training is to take the puppy out frequently and to praise it when the object of the exercise has been achieved.

Infectious Puppy Diseases

The four major infectious diseases from which puppies are especially at risk, and to which unprotected adults are not totally immune, are canine distemper, infectious canine hepatitis, the two forms of leptospirosis known as canicola and icterohaemmorrhagiae, and canine parvovirus; all these can be kept at bay by properly administered vaccines. Puppies will normally receive a degree of immunity from the colostrum contained in the first flow of their mothers' milk. This protection will fade as the puppies get older, but the rate is not constant. Some puppies may lack effective protection by the time they are six weeks old, others may retain enough at twelve weeks of age to block the effect of vaccinations. In normal circumstances the first vaccination should be carried out at eight weeks of age or as soon as possible afterwards, and the second not later than twelve weeks. The puppy should then be fully protected and can then be taken into public places, to puppy training classes and can begin to play a full part in its owner's life.

Most breeders appreciate news of the puppy's progress when it has been in its new home for a few days. There is then an opportunity to discuss any problems which may have arisen or to pose queries which may previously have been overlooked.

Training Classes

If there is a training class nearby, usually run by a canine society but increasingly often by veterinary surgeons, a new owner may enjoy the company of others in the same situation, may exchange experiences and discuss any problems which may arise. There will also be people with some expertise on hand to offer advice and guidance. More importantly, the puppy's range of experience will be further extended, and a start can be made on turning an unruly puppy into a more obedient and civilized creature.

5

Care and Maintenance

While we were writing this book we were invited to take part in a televised discussion in which we would condemn dog owners who decorated their companions with jewelled collars and fancy coats, and whose dogs slept on soft quilts or even – shock! horror! – shared their owner's bed. We declined the invitation. It seems to us that if dogs are properly fed, well housed, given adequate exercise and receive prompt and proper treatment when they are unwell, it is not for us, or anyone else, to be censorious about whether they wear jewelled collars and sleep on their owner's bed.

Preferable to the dog shelf.
(Photo E. Jackson.)

Housing

Accomodation which provides conditions which responsible owners regard as acceptable for themselves is perfectly adequate for even the most fastidious Border Terrier. The essentials are dryness, cleanliness, freedom from draughts, comfort and security. Central heating is not necessary, except for very young and elderly dogs and in times of emergency, though it will certainly be appreciated by all.

Dogs that live in the house should be provided with a bed of their own to which they can retire and in which their privacy and sovereignty will be respected, particularly by younger members of the household who might be inclined to regard a puppy as a toy.

Travelling cages make excellent beds. A dog can be confined in one for safety or privacy, it can then continue to enjoy the use of a secure and familiar bed during stays away from home, and of course such a cage provides a greater level of safety when the dog is travelling. A bed should be large enough for a Border Terrier to stand and lie at full stretch. It should be easily cleaned and, preferably, easily repaired.

Border Terriers which live out of doors can be well accommodated in any one of several makes of kennel to be seen at major shows or advertised in the dog press. They should be large enough to allow a dog or two to move about, and for the owner to gain comfortable access for cleaning. They should be light and airy but well insulated against both winter and summer temperatures. An electricity supply, to provide light or a supplementary source of heat for aged dogs or young puppies, should not be regarded as an unnecessary luxury.

Indoors or out, towels or any one of the synthetic sheepskin fabrics marketed for the purpose make ideal bedding, and clean, white softwood shavings or shredded paper can be added to the list for outdoors. Hay and straw should be avoided for fear of introducing parasites or other irritants into the kennel.

Security

Border Terriers are intended for a job which demands that they should be capable of getting over, under, through or round almost any obstacle. This means that if they develop an urge to be elsewhere, only the very best fence is likely to frustrate that desire. Runs must therefore be made of stout mesh, of a gauge too thick and with apertures too small for even the most determined dog to chew through. Five feet (1.5m) high should be sufficient to outface even the best jumper – although beware dogs which develop an ability to climb: their runs will need a netting roof. Diggers may be frustrated by buried mesh and by hard, paved surfaces.

Border Terriers should not be left to their own devices in a garden which is any less secure than Alcatraz.

Any Border which is confined without entertainment for long periods can be expected to make determined, and doubtless ultimately successful, efforts to escape. If a house, run or kennel becomes a prison, it won't be long before the prisoner either 'goes over the wall' or develops the neurotic behaviour patterns prevalent among animals confined in prison-like zoos. Bored dogs may also be destructive either of their surroundings or, in extreme cases, of themselves. Runs, especially those occupied by puppies, should be stimulating places, furnished with tunnels, tables, logs, any sort of plaything which will entertain and educate the occupants.

Border Terriers are among the breeds which seem particularly attractive to thieves, particularly perhaps those involved in illegal hunting and baiting. It is therefore prudent to ensure that runs and kennels are secure both from within and without.

Training

We are never quite sure whether we train our Borders, whether they train us, or whether we train each other. Dogs certainly seem to train one another. For example, we have one room in our home from which dogs are barred, and puppies very quickly realize that their older companions do not go into that room, at least when we are present – and they, with a little reinforcement from ourselves, quickly learn to accept the house rule.

Lead training should start at an early age using a light slip. There is no need for the harsh check-chains so dear to the hearts of old-fashioned trainers. For unusually recalcitrant dogs there is the Halti, a sort of halter modified for dogs, which usually proves effective without being unnecessarily harsh. Do not use harnesses: not only are these ugly and probably uncomfortable, they are potentially dangerous, because if a Border goes in search of sport a harness may tether it in what might become an underground tomb.

It is important that a dog should return to its owner when ordered to do so. Early training with a reward for obedience will quickly teach it to return on command, whether to a whistle, its name being called or a beckoning hand. Training to more demanding levels of obedience is beyond the scope of this book, although not beyond the ability of Border Terriers to assimilate – even though they are not the first breed which comes to mind when thinking of instant obedience!

Feeding

A mere twenty or so years ago, feeding dogs was often regarded as an art; now, however, it has indisputably become a science which breeders, exhibitors and those who work their terriers in particular need to know something about. Until recently it was almost universally accepted that canned foods, with the addition of some biscuit meal, provided an adequate diet – yet now it is claimed that complete, dry diets offer owners an even simpler and better way of feeding their dogs. In fact, considering the way in which pet food firms continually offer improvements to what had previously been marketed as a perfect diet, it might be suggested that there is no such thing as a diet which is suitable for all dogs, or all dogs in a breed, nor even all dogs in a kennel.

Dogs are individuals, each with slightly different dietary needs depending on their metabolism, their age, the amount of exercise they take and the stress they are called upon to endure. A young, excitable working dog requires a very different diet from an elderly, placid dog which spends much of its life by the fireside.

Owners whose Border Terriers are kept purely as companions can rely with total confidence on many of the range of quite excellent products now on the market; although even with these, some knowledge of the different nutritional demands which are made during the period of growth, in adult health, in sickness and in old age will help to keep their dog in the best possible condition. Some foods are formulated to produce long, silky and shiny coats which are foreign to the breed. Others are intended for dogs with delicate constitutions. Border Terrier owners should be guided by what fellow owners have found to be suitable for the breed.

Exercise

A healthy Border Terrier will take all the exercise it can be given and still come back for more. Ours habitually demand their evening walk even after a long and, for us, arduous day's hunting. It is interesting that after a day at a show, however, both they and their owners are often subdued, the nervous energy expended perhaps having taken more out of them than does physical effort. Otherwise a top class marathon runner could maybe take a Border far enough and fast enough on a lead to give it the sort of exercise it needs, but the rest of us must examine alternatives. We must find an opportunity to give our Borders free exercise, when they can run, jump, turn, tumble and play to their heart's content. Free exercise is the only realistic way to getting a Border really fit, as the feeble-muscled creatures which live their lives in small pens, and for whom exercise consists of an occasional sedate walk on a lead, serve to testify.

If two or more Borders have the opportunity two or three times a day to play their vigorous and sometimes alarmingly rough games together they will sustain a high level of fitness. In the absence of playmates, retrieving a ball or a stick provides an adequate alternative.

Owners should be careful to ensure that they have valid permission before Border Terriers are exercised over farmland, and should be very cautious before exercising them in woodland or, indeed, anywhere where they may inadvertently contravene the Wild Mammals (Protection) Bill. Some wildlife protection groups, welfare organization officers and police are unreasonably overzealous, and seem to assume that anyone with a terrier in such places is there with nefarious intent.

Insurance

Insurance for the first few weeks after a puppy has gone to its new home will usually be available for those bought from reputable breeders. Whether comprehensive insurance cover is maintained thereafter is for the new owner to choose. In our experience it would have been an expensive and unnecessary luxury, although others do not share our experience. Perhaps we have been unusually fortunate. It is important, however, that every Border Terrier is covered for third party risk. A wandering dog may cause a traffic accident, or may injure or kill farm or domestic animals for which its owner will be liable, and legal and compensation costs could add up to many thousands of pounds.

Membership of some Border Terrier breed clubs gives access to block insurance schemes which offer substantial third party insurance. Some household policies provide similar cover. Specialist canine insurance firms also offer a range of policies which not only cover third party risks but also offer protection against unexpected veterinary fees, loss and death. Owners should read the small print with care.

Physical Care

Nails

Dog's nails need to be kept reasonably short. Nails grow at different rates on different dogs, according to the individual's age, constitution, diet, and the quality of exercise it receives. If a dog which moves well, and is given regular and considerable amounts of exercise on hard and abrasive surfaces, its nails may wear down so evenly that they need no other attention – except, of course, for the dew claws which, since they do not, in the normal course of events, come into contact with the ground, will not be affected by exercise. A dog which does not move well may wear nails down differentially so that some will still need attention. Equally a dog which is exercised on grass will not encounter the hard surfaces which will wear nails down, when other attention is needed.

Some authorities recommend that nails are best kept short by filing them. This advice seems to us to stem from someone who has either never had to care for a dog's nails, or not only has the patience of Job but a dog blessed with exceptional patience and tolerance. Regular pedicures using a good pair of nail clippers will keep nails in good order; we prefer the scissor type, though others find that the guillotine type is better. Buy a good quality pair and ensure that they are kept as sharp as possible.

Pelts

Probably the most troublesome parts of any dog to care for are its skin and coat. Although Border Terriers usually, though not invariably, have skins like leather which appear to be resistant to many of the problems encountered in other breeds, and although their coats require no more attention than any caring owner can easily provide, the pelt remains the source of most problems. Border Terriers should have a close-fitting weather-resistant top coat with a texture like a scrubbing brush. Under it should be a thick, soft undercoat and under that a thick, tough skin. Together the two coats and the thick skin form a pelt which provides excellent protection against the worst that a winter's day in Border country can offer.

Any coat which requires frequent, expert attention simply wouldn't provide the necessary degree of protection required for a dog which is essentially a working terrier. The use of knives, scissors, razors and such may create an appearance of smartness, but for those who care to think and see, they either destroy the essential quality of a Border Terrier's coat or hide, or rather attempt to hide, the fact that its natural coat lacks the qualities required to keep a working terrier warm and dry. There should never be any need to employ the services of professional dog groomers, whose methods are likely to produce a dog clipped and trimmed without thought for breed character and in a manner which is more likely to disappoint than please its owner, and may take months to repair.

The removal of dead top coat, using finger and thumb, either regularly in small dribs and drabs, or in one mammoth effort when the coat has begun to shed all over the furniture, is required at regular intervals. The best coats can, with care, be kept virtually permanently in a state which will both repel weather and impress judges. The worst require attention every few weeks if their deficiencies are not to become glaringly apparent; and even then they will either frequently be absent from the ring while they are growing a new coat, or will have to be shown devoid of coat.

Daily grooming creates close and enjoyable contact between dog and owner, and it also provides the opportunity to notice problems before they become intractable and to deal with them while it is a simple matter to do so.

Teeth

Dogs' teeth tend not to be a source of trouble, partly because they don't have to last as long as ours, and partly because dogs tend not to be fed on a sugar-rich diet. Even so, attention to diet, regular inspections, and removal of accumulated tartar will all help to keep a dog's teeth in good order throughout its life. A dog with irregular or otherise incorrect dentition may be expected to experience more dental problems than one which has a correct, even, scissor mouth.

Hard biscuits or dry complete diets have the effect of helping to keep teeth in clean and good condition. Bones, hide chews and plastic toys are not recommended. The power of a Border's jaws is sufficient in time to destroy virtually anything, but its digestive system cannot cope with sharp bone or plastic fragments. Some of the objects sold for dogs to chew may also be contaminated with chemicals commonly used in agriculture which may have a harmful effect.

Identification

From time to time discussion surfaces as to whether an unusually successful and relentlessly shown Border Terrier is one dog, two or perhaps even three, and it is suspected that some dogs may have a corporate rather than an individual existence. As the owners of a bitch which we intended to take to a certain dog, we can remember being advised to take her ourselves otherwise there would be no guarantee as to which dog would actually mate with our bitch. In fact we didn't have the knowledge to identify with certainty each of the dogs in the kennel, and so our bitch went elsewhere. We also know of bitches alleged to have failed to conceive which were seen nursing puppies at the requisite time. And we have seen puppies said to be by one dog which carried peculiarities most often seen on another's puppies.

One old exhibitor's relaxed attitude to life sometimes meant that he arrived at the right show on the wrong day, or at the wrong show on the right day, and we know of one occasion when his error was only discovered after he had won well at a show some miles from the one he had entered. His small kennel produced a steady stream of quality Border Terriers over many years; on one occasion he arrived at a show with three puppy bitches all entered in the same classes, Betty Rumsam designated to handle one, Jean Jackson another and the owner the third, in his estimation the best. Betty and Jean filled the top places in the class, while the owner was among the also-rans. At subsequent shows he avoided the problem by only showing one of his three bitches: the name was constant, but the actual dog could have been any one of the three! However, the owner wasn't trying to cheat anyone, he simply didn't remember which was which! Positive identification would have been an immense help.

Such instances are the rare exception rather than the rule, but they do suggest that the trust on which the Kennel Club registration system relies is not always well placed. Sooner or later all kennel clubs must, in order to protect the integrity of their registration systems as well as for other, incidental reasons, require that every dog which is shown or bred from must be positively identified. From the beginning of 1997 the Irish Kennel Club will make it compulsory for all dogs shown under its rules to be positively identified by tattoo or micro-chip plant.

Many breeders have anticipated enforcement, and already take it upon themselves to have all their puppies individually tattooed before they go to their new homes. The process is simple and causes no more than momentary discomfort. Once a dog has been tattooed, the means to identify it easily throughout the rest of its life can be clearly seen: if it is stolen or strays it can be identified even years after the event. It cannot, in the ring or nursery, be substituted for another or have another substituted for it.

The alternative to tattooing relies on an implanted micro-chip responder carrying information which can subsequently be read by a scanner. However, since scanners are not widely available at present, and are unlikely ever to be available in every situation in which a positive identification is necessary, the use of implants lacks some of the advantages offered by tattooing.

There is a third method of positive identification which relies on the fact that the set of genetic components carried by each dog is unique; it cannot, however, be regarded as an alternative to tattooing or implants, although it is a method which has considerable uses. The method makes use of an analysis of deoxyribonucleic acid (DNA) contained in a sample of skin, hair, blood or other body fluid, other than saliva. Since the make-up of every individual's DNA is unique to that individual, half inherited from the sire and half from the dam, it is possible to use genetic or DNA fingerprinting not only to identify particular individuals but also to identify their parentage. The system is of use when parentage is in doubt or is challenged. It is useful also for AI using stored semen; and as time passes, other uses will doubt-less become apparent.

6

Breeding and Rearing

That most snobbish of nineteenth-century sporting journalists, Nimrod, C.J. Apperley, had something to say about breeding which is not without relevance today:

> It sometimes strikes me that, as hounds improve in beauty, which they certainly do, they lose other more necessary qualities. This is certainly the case, unless they are bred from the very best blood. I conclude this part of my subject, then, by assuring you that, if you attempt to form a pack of fox-hounds yourself, you must not, clever fellow as you are, expect *perfection* under ten years, and that makes a hole even in a young man's life. I can only say it cost me that time to form what I considered a steady and stout pack. Some sorts prove vicious, however highly bred; some unsound, some delicate; and, forasmuch as it requires three years to find out the results of any cross, how favourable soever may be the expectation from it, the breeder of hounds is too often, if not working in the dark, involved in uncertainties and perplexities to no small amount. As is the case with breeding horses, faults of generations back, on one side or the other, will appear; and with hounds, even should the cross suit the first time, there is perplexity again; the produce must be three years old before their real goodness can be verified; and their sire must be at least five or six, as no man would breed from a hound much under three year's standing at his work. Should the cross nick, however, spare no pains to continue it, if circumstances will enable you to do so – that is to say, if the dog and the bitch are within 500 miles of each other.
>
> Now the chief questions for your consideration are – what constitutes a good, and what a faulty hound in his work, and afterwards, his shape and make. The properties of a good hound are soon told. He does his best to find a fox; throws his tongue when he is *sure* he has found him, and not before; gets away *quickly* with the scent so long as it is forward; *stops and turns quickly* when it is not forward; *drives* it to the end *without* dwelling on it, or *tiring*; is *true to the line* without being too eager to get to the head and guide the scent; *sticks to his fox* when he is sinking in a cover, let the cover be ever so strong, which proves his perseverance and stoutness; quite steady from riot in the kennel; not jealous in his work;

good-tempered in the kennel, of a vigorous constitution, and sound from head to foot.

... As respects shape and make, I need not say much on those points to you who have been in the habit of seeing so many good packs, nevertheless you shall have my opinion, as promised. I have always been partial to rather large hounds, provided they are free from lumber and well put together.

We once took some foreign visitors to see a pack of foxhounds in kennels, a quintessential English scene and especially since the kennels in question themselves had considerable architectural merit. However, it was the hounds which most impressed our friends. They had never seen a group of dogs so fit, so beautifully matched in both type and substance and so totally sound. How was this miracle achieved? They turned to us in search of an answer, but while we were frantically searching our minds for a suitable explanation the huntsman piped up:

'Ah', he said, 'we shoot the bad ones.' And what is more, they had been doing so for well over two hundred years. Matings were planned with care, and only the very best of those matings lived to produce the next generation. The process may be unacceptably ruthless for Border Terrier breeders, but there is no denying that breeding only from the best is the best way to produce the best.

Only after a breeder has produced and reared several litters, studied them closely as puppies, and watched them with a discerning and critical eye as they have grown to maturity, may an ability to select puppies begin to be developed. Selection, though, partly at least, informed by simple basic principles, remains a mysterious art which some breeders develop to an almost uncanny degree. Methods vary. Some breeders claim to be best able to recognize future champions at birth, preferably when they are still wet. Others argue, with conviction, that three, five, eight or twelve weeks is undoubtedly the very best time.

The best advice we have had on the subject was offered by Joe Cartledge, a good friend and a world-famous all-rounder. He said that the very best time to pick a puppy was at eleven months and twenty-nine days, unless the month had thirty-one days, in which case the decision could be postponed until the following day.

All that can be done with young puppies is discard those which have obvious faults and keep the rest. But even here one must bear in mind that some faults may disappear as a pup grows. We recall going to see a litter of ten puppies by our Ch. Clipstone Cetchup. None, even several days after birth, were bigger than mice, and they were being reared, in the depths of winter, in an unheated farm building behind a couple of bales of straw. We came away convinced that few would survive such harsh conditions, and equally convinced that any which did so would grow up to be little weedy creatures. In fact all survived, and all grew into Borders whose major fault was that they were far too big!

Learn to select by seeing as many puppies as possible, and always be prepared for surprises. We remember being asked to look at a litter of Border Terriers and seeing the strongest puppies we had ever seen – big, fat, roly-poly things quite different from any Border Terrier puppies we had ever seen. Bowls of food, constantly replenished, were all over the house and we wondered whether this surfeit of food accounted for the puppies' extraordinary development. We revised our view when, as we were taking our leave, a nurse, engaged to care for the breeder's elderly parent during the night, arrived accompanied by a young and vigorous yellow Labrador dog!

At its lowest level, breeding Border Terriers is simply a matter of bringing male and female together at the right time and awaiting the outcome. At a higher level, trying to breed good Border Terriers offers enough challenges, surprises, disappointment and elation to last a lifetime.

Dog breeders in Britain are constrained by both legal and Kennel Club requirements which it is wise to be aware of before any puppies are bred. Analysis of Kennel Club registration figures appears to suggest that those breeds where there is a preponderance of commercial breeders tend to produce most puppies during the early part of the year, presumably to catch summer sales. On the other hand, breeders who have their hopes set on producing puppies good enough to compete in the show ring know that October-born puppies will, at the start of the next show season, be of an age which will give them the best opportunity of a puppy career in showing. But bitches also have a say as to when puppies will be born, and an analysis of Kennel Club registrations over a ten-year period seems to suggest that supposed spring and autumn oestrus peaks may be imaginary.

Legal Requirements

The Breeding of Dogs Act, 1973, requires that all establishments housing more than two breeding bitches must be licensed by the local authority. Not included would be males; neutered females as well as females which are permanently or temporarily prevented from breeding for other reasons; and females outside the age limits which the Kennel Club imposes on bitches producing registered offspring. Breeders who are producing puppies for sale, running a business rather than a hobby, should also be aware of the Pet Animals Act of 1951 and of any subsequent amendments. Anyone who regularly sells pet animals would be wise to ensure that they are exempt from the requirements of the Pet Animals Act.

Only occasional breeders will be exempt from the Breeding of Dogs Act, which requires that:

a)   dogs will at all times be kept in accommodation suitable as regards construction, size of quarters, numbers of occupants, exercising facilities, temperature, lighting, ventilation and cleanliness;
b)   dogs will be adequately supplied with suitable food, drink and bedding material, adequately exercised, and (so far as necessary) visited at suitable intervals;
c)   all reasonable precautions will be taken to prevent and control the spread among dogs of infectious or contagious diseases;
d)   appropriate steps will be taken for the protection of the dogs in the case of fire or other emergency;
e)   all appropriate steps will be taken to secure that the dogs will be provided with suitable food, drink and bedding material and adequately exercised when being transported to or from the breeding establishment.

The requirements are not in themselves unreasonable, but at times have been interpreted in an unreasonable manner by local authority inspectors who are either unaware of the way dogs should be kept, or are under instructions to make life difficult for breeders. For this reason, as well as because some local authorities demand punitive licence fees, many breeders with small kennels have not sought registration. However, in 1991 an amendment to the Act gave local authority inspectors the right of entry to premises which they had reason to believe were being used for breeding dogs. This right of entry was confined to kennels and outbuildings and did not include domestic premises.

When the Breeding of Dogs Act first made its appearance in 1973, one well known breeder applied for a licence. Like all good breeders the kennel's owner reared puppies in the house. The arrangement, however, appeared not to meet with the unqualified approval of the inspector who had called to assess the kennel's suitability. He suggested that it was not hygienic to have puppies in a kitchen. 'Oh, it's all right,' explained the breeder, 'I always wash my hands before I touch them.'

Apart from controls imposed by the law, the Kennel Club also exerts its own forms of control, and these are binding on everyone who makes use of Kennel Club services. Only in extreme circumstances, and when prior permission has been given, will the Kennel Club register puppies from bitches which are less than twelve months old. A similar embargo exists for puppies whose mothers are over seven years old. The restrictions are intended to prevent breeding bitches being abused and as such are welcome, although there is no physiological reason why bitches under twelve months and over seven years should not be bred from.

A bitch may be mated at the first season after her first birthday, though in practice show bitches may not be mated until they have enjoyed success in the ring. They may be mated at any time up to three or even four years old, though beyond that time a bitch may be getting too old, her bones and temperament too set, to face the prospect of rearing her first litter.

Quality

No one who genuinely intends to breed good Border Terriers would ever think of breeding from stock which was not out of the very top drawer, physically and temperamentally sound, and typical of the breed – though of course, each of us might define what is top quality in slightly different terms.

A good friend of ours was once severely castigated by an enthusiastic newcomer to the breed, whose strong opinions, based on little knowledge, were broadcast with almost evangelical zeal: 'You should not breed from bitches you don't think are good enough to show.'

To which he replied: 'But you show bitches I don't think are good enough to breed from!'

Appearance

Change in the appearance of domestic livestock is inevitable without a positive and determined effort to prevent it. Different breeds adopt different attitudes towards change: some strive to prevent it, some allow it to happen, and some actively encourage it. Among domesticated animals change is the product of the contents of the available gene pool and of the process of selection employed by breeders.

Appearance is also partly a product of environmental factors, the way dogs are cared for, and as these conditions change, so will the animal itself. In dogs probably the two most important factors which have contributed to change are improved nutritional standards and more effective control over internal parasites, both of which result in bigger, stronger and healthier dogs. If dogs from the past, Liddesdale Bess or Teri say, were to be born now and reared by the methods currently available, they would not, as adults, look like they did having been reared by the less sophisticated methods available before 1920.

In domesticated animals, changes due to inherited factors are likely to be less dramatic, perhaps even imperceptible, in a large population than in a smaller one. Because Britain has a larger population of Border Terriers than anywhere else in the world, change is likely to be slower, whether for good or ill. However, even in Britain the population is not so large that an individual, frequently used dominant stud-dog could not have a major effect on a significant proportion of the breed. The effect of an individual may be seen more dramatically when its use is confined to a small area and especially to certain kennels.

It is undeniable that Border Terriers have changed since they were first recognized; whether this change is good or bad, accidental or deliberately engineered, we leave others to decide. However, the extent of change has been largely controlled by the fact that the breed has remained in close contact with its work. While the breed remains **essentially a working terrier**, no changes which might take place, whether by accident or deliberately, can be acceptable if they reduce the breed's ability to work. Work, then, has exerted control over change, but that control, during the last few years, appears to be less effective than was once the case. Perhaps some breeders no longer regard the ability to work as important, perhaps some no longer understand what is needed in order to satisfy the demands exerted by work. Will the consequence be that the rate of change will accelerate, taking the breed in a direction which earlier breeders would regard as unacceptable?

Genetics

Since the Czechoslovakian monk, Gregor Johann Mendel, discovered the basic laws of inheritance in 1860, the science of genetics has unravelled many more of the laws which govern the way in which physical and mental attributes are inherited. Scientists have concentrated their principal interest on animals and plants which can be made more profitable by the application of a knowledge of genetics, and as a consequence dogs have been relatively ignored. Breeds which have a wide range of coat colours or which have the misfortune to have inherited disease tend to be the ones to which breeders devote most attention regarding the study of genetics.

'I'm glad,' said one very successful Border Terrier breeder to us, 'that Border Terriers have fewer genetics than other breeds.'

Border Terriers have a very limited colour range, and generally breeders are prepared to accept whatever comes rather than to breed for a particular colour. Further, the breed has few inherited problems, and these are mostly both relatively rare and trivial. However, they will be kept in their place only if breeders are aware of the existence of problems in their breeding stock, face them honestly and take whatever steps are necessary to avoid reproducing them. Fortunately British Border Terrier breeders have a sufficiently large pool of breeding stock to enable them to avoid breeding from any animals about which there may be doubts, no matter how slight. Those overseas are perhaps less fortunate.

There are no Border Terriers which are vital to the breed's future. Some have made important contributions to the breed, but it would not have been catastrophic if even these had not been bred from. There is no need to breed from Border Terriers which are not of the very top quality in every respect.

Line-Breeding and Inbreeding

These are not scientific terms with accepted, precisely defined meanings: they are sometimes used, in an Alice-in-Wonderlandish sort of way, to mean all sorts of different things. Both terms imply that an individual dog appears more than once in a pedigree, and it might be convenient to define inbreeding as the appearance of a parent in earlier generations, and line-breeding simply as the repeated appearance of a more distant ancestor.

The old breeders whose aim was to produce sound, tough and sensible working terriers made use of the advantages which inbreeding offers. They avoided its perils by their ability to identify outstanding stock and by a rigorous, even ruthless, process of selection. Primitive methods of rearing and the absence of protective vaccines also eliminated weak individuals. Unwise modern breeders often apply a far less stringent process of selection. Faults may be multiplied by close breeding, and blame is placed not on an inability to select breeding stock but on inbreeding itself.

Having selected a suitable animal to which it is intended to inbreed, it is then useful to have some means by which the degree of inbreeding can be measured and thus controlled. Wright's 'coefficient of inbreeding' provides a means by which the degree of inbreeding to a particular individual can be calculated, but it involves some rather tedious calculations. We have reduced these calculations to tabular form (see Appendix 5) so that it is possible, by reference to the table, to see precisely what degree of inbreeding exists within any four generation pedigree.

Why inbreed at all? There are two reasons for inbreeding: the first is quite simply that in a numerically small population it is impossible to avoid; and the second is that it offers the best means to perpetuate the desirable qualities of a particular specimen.

Inbreeding does not introduce characteristics which the breeding stock does not carry, though the characteristics may not always be apparent. However, over time it does tend to reduce fertility and vitality. Inbreeding is a sharp tool, capable of doing as much harm as good, and perhaps even more. For this reason a thorough knowledge of pedigrees is essential to successful inbreeding. Inbreeding cannot itself discriminate between desirable and undesirable characteristics: that is the breeder's task. The breeder who is blind to faults in his own stock or to qualities in other stock may well find that inbreeding not only offers little of value, but may be a rapid road to ruin.

Making Arrangements

Well before a bitch from which there is an intention to breed, comes into season, her owner should have selected a suitable mate for her, sought and received the stud-dog owner's permission to use the dog, found out what the stud fee will be, and what arrangements the stud-dog's owner will require. If your bitch is not up to the standard he/she requires, or if, in his/her opinion, her breeding is unlikely to be compatible with the dog's, you may have to look elsewhere or even abandon the idea of breeding from her.

In Britain it is customary to pay a stud fee, usually somewhat more than half the cost of a puppy, but for the most popular dogs – though not necessarily the best – as much or more than the cost of a puppy. In practice, stud-dog owners can set the fee at any level they like, and the owners of bitches have the choice of paying it or looking elsewhere. Do not entertain any arrangements which involve giving up any of the puppies.

The stud fee is payable at the time of and immediately after the first mating, and is not returnable if the bitch fails to conceive. It is the dog owner's responsibility to offer the services of a fertile dog, although even the most fertile dog cannot impregnate an infertile bitch or one which is not in the process of ovulation. We have a friend who deals with those who report that the bitch will be ready on Wednesday but prefer to bring her to the dog on the previous Sunday or the following Saturday simply by asking: 'Do you want your bitch to have pups or just to have sex?' The question makes the point admirably.

Some stud-dog owners will offer a second service, especially for maiden bitches, but in reality if the first mating is a good one a second should not be necessary. A free return service is not a right. The offer will invariably be subject to the dog's continued availability and to veterinary confirmation of the bitch's fertility. If the offer is made it should be confirmed in writing.

Care of the Stud-Dog

The care of a stud-dog is every bit as specialized a craft as the care of a brood-bitch. Dogs to be offered at public stud must, of course, be of first class quality. Many years ago Raymond Oppenheimer told us that bad dogs never make good stud-dogs, and he was right: stud-dogs must be confident, tolerant, fit and in good health, and they must, of course, be fertile.

A dog which is intended for stud work should not be reared in isolation. He needs the opportunity to play with other dogs and to practise his technique. When he is about a year old his education should be completed by an introduction to an accommodating in-season bitch, in the circumstances in which future performances will take place; and the more wanton she is, the better! He should be encouraged to mate her, and assisted to do so by his owner. Once penetration has taken place the two should be gently restrained. A stud-dog which will accept help will be better able to mate difficult bitches than one which is intolerant of assistance – though it could be argued that unwilling bitches should not be mated. Only when the dog's proving litter has been born should he be offered at stud.

We prefer to accommodate the couple in a large and secure grass run where they can indulge in fore-play. Other breeders have well appointed, comfortable sheds for the purpose; some prefer to have the mating take place on a table. Stud-dogs tend to be creatures of routine, and become excited when they enter the familiar routine.

A good stud-dog will mate a willing bitch within a few minutes of being introduced to her. Failure to do so suggests either that he has not been well trained or that the bitch is not ready to be mated.

Sire Selection

All sorts of infallible systems exist for choosing precisely the right sire for any particular bitch: using some particular male relative, her grandsire or her half-brother are favoured by some; others like to use a dog which is out of a female relative. In reality, the numerous infallible systems for breeding top quality puppies are no more reliable than those which are used to select winning racehorses, score draws or the right sequence of lottery numbers. Thus the nearest or cheapest dog can be selected on the grounds of convenience or economy, whereas some breeders will beat a path to the kennel door of the

Ch. Dandyhow Shady Knight when full of years.

current top winning dog. However, these rely on luck rather than good judgement.

A sire should be chosen not just for his own qualities and his pedigree, but on his proven ability to produce top quality puppies, preferably to bitches which are related to your own. If he has already done this, your chance of also producing top quality puppies would appear to be appreciably enhanced.

Brood-Bitches

Any bitch from which it is intended to breed must be well bred. She must be healthy; she must have no glaring faults; she must show no sign of hereditary disease, and be unlikely to carry any hidden defects. Any bitch which has any serious temperamental or physical defects, or which is in any way untypical of the breed should not be bred from.

Once a bitch has reached about eighteen months of age she can then be mated to the most suitable and best available dog. Her first litter might be delayed for another year or even longer without untoward effects, but it should not be delayed until advancing age begins to erode her health and vigour.

Proud mum. (Photo. Anne Cumbers.)

The decision to breed should be anticipated. Thus care should be taken when buying a female puppy that she is likely to grow into a bitch fit to be bred from: this means buying a well bred, well reared, sound and healthy puppy which is the product of parents with similar good qualities.

Bitches are fertile for only a short period – sometimes for no more than a few hours – during their cyclical season. A normal Border bitch will usually come into season when she is about six months old. In a few cases the first season may be delayed until the bitch is over twelve months old, but a longer delay should be treated as an indication that something is amiss.

Subsequent seasons will occur at more or less regular intervals. However, variations can be produced by stress, or they may be caused by illness or injury, even by a change of home, temporary or otherwise, or by the weather – seasons are, to some extent at least photogenically, induced. Even the presence of other bitches in season can induce a season – which breeders refer to as the 'me, too, syndrome.'

Irregular, infrequent or unusual seasons should be regarded as an indication that the bitch may not readily conceive and possibly, since the tendency may be inherited, as a reason for not breeding from her at all.

Fertility

There was a time when it seemed necessary only to rub two Border Terriers together in order to produce puppies. Nowadays, however, things sometimes seem to be slightly more difficult. Whether this is the symptom of some change in dogs generally; the breed itself; of attempts to breed from animals with reduced fertility, or of some other factor, we are unable to say. There is evidence which suggests that inbred dogs are less fertile than those which have a more open pedigree. There is also evidence which suggests that females of a family in which monorchids or cryptorchids are to be found are likely to have a reduced level of fertility. We suspect, however, that by far the most frequent causes of infertility are bringing the dog and bitch together at the wrong time, and lack of proper subsequent care for the bitch.

Eyes not yet open.

95

Seasons

A bitch's season consists of two quite distinct phases, pro-oestrus and oestrus. Each lasts, on average, for about nine or ten days, though the variation between individual bitches and even between an individual bitch's seasons may be considerable. At pro-oestrus the bitch may become restive and even irritable, and she may urinate frequently in an instinctive effort to advertise her condition to likely suitors. A normally adjusted bitch will flirt with her companions, and they may take an increasing interest in her developing condition. Her vulva will swell and will emit a blood-infused discharge, though if the bitch is scrupulous in cleaning herself this may not be apparent unless she is carefully observed.

After nine or ten days, pro-oestrus gives way to oestrus, the season proper, during which the bitch should be receptive to a dog and should be fertile. Her vulva will become soft and spongy and the blood will disappear from the discharge. She may become increasingly flirtatious, even making determined efforts to escape in order to find a mate. She will be very attractive to males which will make every effort to reach her.

Ovulation occurs during oestrus, and mating should be timed to coincide with this unseen event. If the bitch is normally adjusted she may show her readiness by provocatively curling her tail and arching her back after a bout of coquettish behaviour. She may behave indiscriminately in this manner towards dogs, bitches, her owner and even the family cat. Breeders refer to the behaviour as 'standing', and as soon as possible after such behaviour is seen she must mated. Some bitches will remain fertile for a few days, some only for a matter of hours, but for all there will be a short period of optimum fertility, after which, as eggs cease to be available for fertilization, mating will produce a reduced number of puppies.

In an unmated bitch, or in one which has failed to conceive, oestrus will usually give way to metoestrus and then to anoestrus, during which time she ceases to be fertile and returns to her customary condition until the next cyclical advent of pro-oestrus.

Repeat Matings

The temptation to repeat an extraordinarily successful mating – engendered by the hope that lightning may strike twice in the same place – is an understandable one, but it is one which, especially in a small kennel, might best be resisted. Exceptional success is, by its very nature, unlikely to be repeated, and especially by ageing parents. Even if a second or third litter does match or even surpass the quality of the first and gains success in the ring, nothing will have been achieved which will enable the kennel to develop its breeding programme. The second litter will not contribute anything to the breeding stock which is not present in the first litter, and the kennel's genetic pool, already smaller than can be easily managed, is being even further restricted.

Pregnancy

Pregnancy follows a successful mating. It lasts, on average, for sixty-three days, though in our experience it tends to be shorter than the average for all breeds. Puppies born five or six days before full term have a much reduced chance of survival, and those whose birth is delayed two or three days beyond full term may become too big to be born naturally. Unusually small puppies and those in big litters also have a reduced chance of survival and should receive special care.

For about two or three weeks after mating, fertilized eggs, zygotes, float freely about the uterus. At this stage they are very vulnerable and might be aborted if the bitch is subjected to trauma or stress. For this reason she should quickly return to her customary life after she has been mated. Visits to shows, where infection may be picked up and where she will be under some stress, are best avoided. It may be significant that bitches, even some of the most successful the breed has produced, which are shown after they have been mated tend to have poor fertility records.

After about three weeks the zygotes implant on the uterus wall where they grow, in a matter of just a few weeks, from no more than a few cells into puppies capable of independent existence. Even during the early days after implantation the embryos remain vulnerable to stress and may be aborted or reabsorbed if conditions become stressful. Vets who spay bitches which have never produced puppies frequently discover scars on the uterus wall, a condition which shows that puppies have been implanted but not carried to full term.

Pregnancy Diagnosis

Once a bitch has been mated, the owner awaits the first positive signs that she may be in whelp with whatever patience can be mustered. The temptation to subject the bitch to some form of pregnancy diagnosis may become irresistible – but be aware that although the procedure may satisfy the owner's curiosity, it may also subject the bitch to unnecessary stress and cannot, in any case, guarantee that the puppies will be carried to full term.

By the end of the third week, skilled and gentle palpation of the uterus may reveal pea-sized objects: these are the developing embryos. If they can't be found, the bitch may not be in whelp; alternatively she may be too muscular or tense to allow successful palpation, or she may be carrying her puppies in an inaccessible part of the uterus, or the palpation may not be sufficiently skilled.

By about the fifth or sixth week the distensions will disappear under surrounding fluid and tissue; by this time, however, the bitch's teats will have begun to swell, and her stomach will have begun to become enlarged. At this stage radiograph examination can focus on the embryos developing skeletons and can provide a positive diagnosis of pregnancy. It may also be possible to hear foetal heartbeats. Examination of foetal fluids, blood and ultra-sound examination are other methods which are also increasingly being used.

The best any method can achieve is confirmation that the bitch is in whelp when the examination took place. None can predict the likelihood of reabsorbtion or of spontaneous abortion, both of which become more likely if the bitch is subjected to stress, possibly even the sort of stress produced by the examination itself. Nor can any method demonstrate with absolute certainty that a bitch has failed to conceive, and whatever the diagnosis, any breeder with a spark of sense or concern for the bitch would continue to treat her as though she were in whelp. We have known of bitches which had confidently been pronounced not in whelp which were then either subjected to stress which produced a spontaneous abortion, or went on to produce puppies in circumstances so unsuitable that all were lost.

Whelping

The first signs that whelping is imminent presage a time which, for caring breeders, is fraught with excitement, anxiety, hope and sometimes disappointment. As we have said already, in our experience all breeds including Borders tend to whelp before the full sixty-three days of an average canine pregnancy have elapsed. They also seem to whelp at night more often than during the day. Responsible breeders will keep their diaries clear around the time when the birth is due, because it is important that someone is to hand capable of dealing effectively with any emergency which may arise.

The first sign that birth is imminent will be that the bitch becomes restless, investigating places, usually unsuitable, in which to give birth. If she has already been acclimatized to the place in which it is intended that she should give birth this process may be less apparent. She may refuse food and urinate frequently. She may resent the attentions of her companions, who, for their part, often exhibit an increased interest in her condition. If the breeder has kept a record of the bitch's normal temperature, generally about 101.5°F, a slight but significant fall will also give an indication that birth is imminent.

If the breeder has not already assembled everything which may be needed during the birth, now is the time to calm excitement and apprehension by making quite sure that preparations are complete. Clean towels, a clean cardboard box lined with a towel, a supply of clean newspapers, clean bedding, a pair of sharp scissors, whatever the breeder may rely on to remain alert during what may be a prolonged vigil and, in anticipation of the worst, the veterinary surgeon's telephone number should all be in readiness.

The breeder should maintain an unobtrusive surveillance throughout what is about to ensue. His/her presence and timely action to assist the bitch and her puppies can, quite literally, mean the difference between life and death.

Eventually the bitch will begin to arrange her bed to her liking. If she is bedded on newspapers, which are easily shredded and arranged by her and as easily replaced by the breeder as they become soiled, she will make a comfortable, if messy nest. She will then proceed to stage two of the process, which may last for as little as a quarter of an hour or as long as an hour; any longer, however should give cause for the beginnings of alarm. During this period she will pant, her facial expression will be strained, she will be restless and as the process proceeds will begin to have contractions. These exhibit themselves in the form of straining which arches the back, lifts the head for a short period before subsiding, only to be repeated with increasing vigour as the first birth becomes imminent.

At the start of the third stage, the birth itself, the foetal bag appears and quite soon afterwards the puppy is expelled, followed by its still-attached placenta. At this stage a maiden bitch may show some understandable bewilderment and, if so, the breeder might offer assistance, first by massaging the umbilical cord towards the puppy, and then severing it, preferably with a jagged cut about an inch (2.5cm) from the puppy. The placenta contains a substance which stimulates the production of milk and should be left for the bitch to eat. The puppy can then be thoroughly towelled both to stimulate it and to dry it – more puppies are lost from hypothermia than by any other cause.

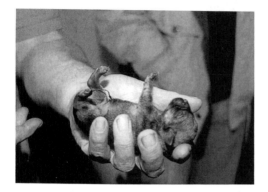

New born.

By this time the bitch will have returned to stage two in preparation for the birth of the next puppy: contractions may begin again almost immediately, or she may rest quietly, in which case she may be given the puppy to nurse. If her bed has become badly soiled a layer of clean newspaper can be quietly provided. When contractions begin again, the first puppy may be placed in the cardboard box, covered to retain heat, and the birth of the second puppy awaited.

The process is repeated, and may be repeated up to seven or eight, even ten times, though four or five is more usual before the birth is complete. As the bitch becomes increasingly tired the intervals between births will get longer, and the breeder should keep a watchful eye to ensure that progress is maintained; exhaustion may induce inertia which will require immediate veterinary attention if the remaining puppies are to survive.

Eventually the birth will be complete, and the bedding can be changed while the bitch is enjoying a nutritious drink: we use an isotonic fluid which is nourishing, easily assimilated and prevents scouring; others use a glucose and water solution. If all is well, the bitch will now be contentedly nursing her brood and the breeder can succumb to the effects of a long and stressful ordeal. If all it not well, however, further stress must be expected. The following developments call for outside assistance:

If, after giving every sign that birth is imminent, the bitch fails to

Day olds.

produce her puppies or to do so reasonably expeditiously, veterinary assistance must be urgently sought.

Sometimes prior to the birth, but more often when she is nursing puppies, the bitch may become unduly restless, panting, shivering and shaking: if she shows these symptoms she may be in the first stages of eclampsia, or milk fever, and will urgently require an injection of calcium if the condition is to be prevented from progressing to ataxia, paralysis, coma and death.

The first stage may fail to proceed to contractions: this is called primary uterine inertia, often a consequence of carrying a single puppy or a very large litter, and in this case a stimulant injection may be urgently required to save the puppies' lives.

Contractions may also fail to lead to a birth, in which case there may be some physical obstruction; if this is a malpresented puppy, a skilled breeder may be able to solve the problem and so allow birth to proceed. If, however, the problem is caused by a small bitch straining to give birth to unusually large puppies, surgical assistance will be urgently needed.

An excitable bitch or one which has been unreasonably disturbed by a thoughtless audience may become neurotically attentive to her puppies and in the process do them actual physical harm. She should be kept under close supervision, and the breeder should seriously consider the possibility that her puppies should be removed and hand-reared.

It is not unusual for bitches to have a discharge from the vulva for some days, and perhaps weeks or even months, after the birth. If this remains clean and inoffensive there need be no cause for alarm; but if it shows any sign of becoming putrid it is possible that foetal matter has been retained, in which case veterinary attention is required.

Contented pups.

Rearing

After the birth a bitch may be reluctant to leave her puppies for some days, although she should be encouraged to do so. At first she should be fed on small, frequent bland meals; after a few days the amount can be increased and the content changed for one of the diets specifically formulated for nursing bitches. As the puppies grow, so will her appetite until she is eating up to three or even four times her normal intake.

The behaviour of puppies is perhaps the best indicator that all is well or that something is amiss. Healthy puppies, sucking vigorously, sleeping contentedly in an untidy huddle or chirping in obvious satisfaction present a very different picture from those which are crying hungrily, searching restlessly or lying torpidly in a corner of the nest. In this case, if the bitch has a good milk supply and the temperature is adequate, some other explanation for the problem must be sought. A mild antibiotic coupled with supplementary feeding may be required, but even then the breeder must prepare to face the death of at least some of the litter.

Border Terrier bitches tend to make rough and ready mothers, giving their puppies adequate,but not over-solicitous attention. After a couple of weeks they may visit them only to feed them, and after about three weeks only to see if they have left any of the food which by now the breeder will be providing. As with all other aspects of feeding, weaning preparations are now available which ease what used to be a troublesome process, and which provide for all the nutritional needs of growing puppies. Puppies at this age grow more quickly than a human baby and so their nutritional needs are appreciable; and promising puppies can be ruined by an inadequate or inappropriate diet.

Food is not all they need. If they are to grow into well socialized, well adjusted, confident adults they need a stimulating environment, challenges, the opportunity to explore, to extend their experiences and, most of all, the constant and kindly attention of people. This last may even have begun at birth when their breeder dried and stimulated them, and it should continue throughout their period in the nest: handling them, talking to them, cleaning them after feeds, all such attention helps them to learn to trust people and to want to please them.

Family group.

In our view Border Terriers are perhaps more needful of careful socialization than some other breeds if they are to become well adjusted adults. Perhaps this is why breeders who do not provide this attention are often less successful than those who do. Summer puppies which can play, exercise and explore out of doors are far easier to cope with than those born in winter. A run furnished with boxes, tunnels and appropriate toys will encourage them to develop physically and mentally – but nothing, absolutely nothing, is as important as the breeder's constant attention.

It is often said that puppies are great time wasters: in truth, the time spent with a litter of puppies is never wasted.

Naming

The business of naming and registering puppies may either take place as soon as the breeder is confident that the puppies are thriving, or it may be delayed so that the purchasers can select their own puppy's name for themselves.

Nowadays it is usual for breeders to register an affix with the Kennel Club. The affix, which may be exclusive to an individual or shared between partners, is unique and is protected on payment of an annual fee. The name is used as a prefix on dogs bred by the owner, and may be attached as a suffix to dogs which have been bought in.

Both the affix and the puppy's individual name should preferably reflect the breed's sporting background, or at least not be at odds with it. Nor should the name suggest that the puppy's character or conformation are other than typical of the breed. The Kennel Club will reject any names which are obscene, disrespectful, use canine terms, coincide with a registered affix, repeat the name of a dog already in the Stud Book, employ numerals, have more than twenty-four letters, begin with a single letter word or, nowadays, consist of a solitary word.

Complying with all the restrictions is not always easy. It is not very long since we tried to register a puppy as Clipstone Champagne, having forgotten that Champagne was already registered as an affix. The Kennel Club took it upon themselves to register the puppy as Clipstone Baby Cham, but allowed us another choice after we had pointed out that we did not regard Baby Cham as an adequate alternative to champagne! Callum, Latin for 'thick-skinned', was surely named in an inspired moment, as was Ch. Troglodyte, a cave dweller.

The names of the litter brother and sister Ch. What Fettle and Ch. Gay Fine cleverly encapsulated a northern greeting. George Ion employed the Cumbrian name for an oak apple when he named Ch. Yak Bob.

Some breeders use the same initial letter when naming a litter, and then move on to the next letter in the alphabet for the next litter. Some try to use the same initials for all their puppies; some use themes. In fact the process of naming puppies can be as simple or as complicated as the breeder wishes to make it!

Three generations. (Photo. Anne Cumbers.)

As far as pet names are concerned there are no restrictions, but it is as well to remember that the name will almost certainly have to be called aloud, and that more than two syllables become difficult. If an owner has more than one dog it will avoid confusion if their names are phonetically distinct – though all will probably respond to each other's names for fear of missing something of interest!

The best toys are those you find for yourself. (Photo. Anne Cumbers.)

105

Brackens, Rustys and Sandys abound in the breed, and we have met several Herbies, only one of which was prepared to admit that this had been shortened from Herbaceous. It was probably inevitable that Brussel Sprout, whose kennel name included his breeder's initials, should be known to his family and friends as 'Veg'!

Buying and Selling

In this increasingly litigious world, a sharpened commercial attitude among some breeders, and the fact that purchasers are protected by both general and specific legislation, has meant that the process of buying and selling puppies becomes ever more hazardous. The law prohibits dogs being sold in the street or in any public place. From time to time, however, puppies and older dogs are offered for sale at shows and other events – but to do this is illegal, and places both the vendor and the show organizer on the wrong side of the law. Furthermore, if animals are offered for sale from a private dwelling or associated buildings as part of a business, this may bring into play the Pet Animals Act, 1951; this Act requires that pet shop owners must be licensed by the local authority.

Doleful youngster.
(Photo. Anne Cumbers.)

The law in general takes the view that buyers must take such precautions as are necessary to ensure that what they buy is likely to fulfil its intended purpose. However, if a buyer specifically states that the puppy is being bought for a particular purpose – for work, show or breeding – and the vendor sells the puppy knowing of its intended use, he may, if the puppy turns out to be unsuitable for its intended purpose, have a claim under the Sale of Goods Act, 1979.

7

A Border a Day . . .

Anti-dog sentiments, which feed on ignorance and prejudice but which in themselves are nothing new, seem almost to be reaching epidemic proportions. Yet the benefits to be derived from dogs are nowadays not merely recognized by biased owners, but are also increasingly recognized and even measured by scientists. The use of dogs to guide the blind, to alert the deaf, and for search and rescue are well known – but less well known areas of use are continually being found. Andrew Edney presented a paper at the World Veterinary Congress which gave details of early research into the use of dogs to recognize the early signs of epileptic seizures.

The companionship provided by a dog offers security, relief from loneliness, interest and a reason for pride. But dog ownership offers more tangible benefits, too: for example Warwick Anderson, a doctor at the Baker Institute for Medical Research in Melbourne, set out to show that there was no relationship between pets and health. He studied 8,000 people, delving into their diets, exercise, drinking habits, family history and pet ownership, and found that in spite of the fact that pet owners had a slightly higher intake of fried food and of alcohol (neither totally unknown among Border Terrier owners), they tended

John Renton's Ch. Happy Day.

to have lower blood pressure and lower plasma triglyceride levels than non-pet owners. He found, too, that the blood chemistry of pet owners as well as their physiological profiles made them less likely to contract heart disease than non-pet owners. Dr Anderson concluded that 'if a pharmaceutical company marketed a drug that could produce these results, they would have a world breakthrough'.

At any canine event, people long past the time when they might be expected to be indulging in demanding competitive events, are to be seen vying energetically with people half their age and less. But in doing this they are looking forwards, with ambition, enthusiasm and interest intact. One of the most telling examples of this which we saw was during our last visit to John Renton, who, in spite of being a very old and sick man, was still planning his breeding programme. He had decided that he needed to do something to improve coats, and had devised a cunning plan whereby we would act as his agents and buy a dog puppy from Bobby Benson's Daletyne kennel, whose coats were second to none. John would then make use of this puppy to improve coats in his own kennel. Sadly John died before a suitable puppy became available and so the Machiavellian scheme was never put into effect.

We don't know of any breed which provides access to quite such an extensive and varied range of legitimate interests as do Border Terriers. Unfortunately the breed's sporting proclivities also provide access to illegal activities in which no one with the slightest claim to humanity would indulge. These we will ignore as unworthy of comment.

Legitimate sporting activities have already been discussed – what remains is to consider the range of other activities to which recognition and more recent developments have provided access.

Shows

Dog shows of one sort or another have been taking place in Britain at least since the end of the eighteenth century, when John Warde ran hound shows at his home at Squerries in Kent. Small, localized shows run by hunts, by the emergent agricultural societies and in the back rooms of urban public houses were well established before the creation of an extensive and reasonably efficient railway system enabled larger shows with national appeal to develop. During the 1860s a number of societies were founded to run shows whose efforts are still an important part of the British show scene.

Sharing a bench.
(Photo. E. Jackson)

After 1873, when the Kennel Club was founded, the majority of shows were run under well defined rules and, when Kennel Club authority had developed, were administered by a strong regulatory body. Showing dogs had become established as a pastime which attracted exhibitors from all levels of society and of all ages. However, until recognition in 1920, Border Terriers were largely confined to shows in the Border region which existed outside the Kennel Club system. After 1920 they were free to take part in both Kennel Club and non-regulated shows.

Showing dogs is a competitive activity which attracts people from all walks of life and from every age group. Whether for good or bad, it relies on the opinion of one individual to decide the winners, and of course the hope and aim is to win. However, those for whom winning is the *only way* that dog shows become enjoyable would be well advised to avoid them. No one has ever had a dog of any breed good enough to win *all* the time, and in Border Terriers the variations in fitness, coat quality, interpretation of the Standard and a thousand-and-one other factors combine to ensure that winners are seldom pre-determined – though some people are inclined to lay claim to a degree of prescience.

Showing dogs offers an opportunity to see some of the best dogs the breed has to offer, to mix with people who share a common enthusiasm for the breed, to make new friends and to travel to new places.

Two quite different sorts of show are available for Border Terriers: there are hunt or working terrier shows, often run by a hunt or hunt supporters' club or, increasingly nowadays, by country fairs; and there are shows run under Kennel Club rules. Many owners support both

Intense competition.

types of show, savouring the often considerable differences and deriving enjoyment from both.

Hunt and working terrier shows grew out of the hound shows which began in the 1850s, but began to approach their present level of popularity only in the post-war years. About five hundred such shows now take place each summer. Some will attract no more than a handful of Border Terriers, while at the most popular the numbers will rival even those which are attracted by breed club events.

Working terrier shows are open to any terrier which can be described as a working terrier – though in practice this eliminates the majority of recognized terrier breeds. In fact it is unusual to find any recognized terrier breeds other than Bedlington Terriers, Parson Jack Russell Terriers and, of course, Border Terriers. A very limited range of classes are usually on offer, with seldom more than two, divided between the sexes, for each working terrier breed. Dogs do not need to be registered with the Kennel Club nor even to be the product of pedigree parents:

Only at the largest shows does judging begin before lunch. Entries, except for shows run by country fairs, are usually taken on the day, and entry fees are comparatively modest. Judging is generally in the hands of a specialist working terrier judge, and sometimes a panel of judges whose deliberations provide an additional spectacle of interest in the centre of the ring. The judging procedure is governed partly by a tolerant tradition and partly by the judge's own preferences. Equally decisions are based on what the judge himself – only very occasionally is this *her*self – regards as an ideal working terrier, and rather less on characteristics which breeders might regard as essential to their breed.

Hunt terrier shows have no central authority to set standards or settle disputes, and as a consequence they vary enormously in quality. The best are quite excellent, the worst offer an experience which few would wish to undergo a second time.

The informality of hunt terrier shows is one of their charms.

Exemption shows which are licensed by the Kennel Club but exempted from compliance with its show regulations, might in some respects be regarded as a halfway house between hunt terrier shows and shows run under KC rules. Classification is restricted, and classes specifically for Border Terriers are never provided. There are usually more novelty classes than regular ones, and although the competitive edge can sometimes be quite sharp, these events are best regarded as a source of fun allied to a chance to support a charity and as a training ground for youngsters. Exhibits at exemption shows are not required to be registered with the Kennel Club.

Shows run under Kennel Club or Irish Kennel Club rules are open only to exhibits registered with the relevant bodies. In addition, the Irish Kennel Club requires that all exhibits must be positively identified in an approved manner by tattoo or implanted micro-chip.

Kennel Club shows offer a hierarchy of events ranging from small ones, entry to which is restricted to dogs that have not won awards counting towards the title of Champion, up through shows which are open to all, and onwards to Championship Shows at which awards on offer count towards the title of Champion. The range caters for all levels of ambition on the part of exhibitors, and for a wide range of quality on the part of dogs. As far as most Border Terrier exhibitors are concerned, a win at breed club shows, and particularly the breed clubs' Championship Shows, represents the pinnacle of achievement.

Show Dogs

Not only must show dogs of any breed be sound, fit and typical specimens of their breed, they must also enjoy showing. The purpose of any dog show is for the judge to find, on the day, what he or she regards as the best dogs. This does not simply mean the dog which is in best coat or condition, or which walks or poses best, but the best dog overall. Of course, conditioning and presentation are important, and so too is ringcraft, but these can only be regarded as the means by which the overall quality of the dog itself is revealed.

Too much!

There is a fallacy, commonly paraded by people who know nothing about dog shows, that show dogs are highly strung, neurotic creatures. However, such a dog could not possibly be expected to withstand the tests which dog shows impose. Show dogs, especially Border Terriers, must have the sort of temperament which will enable them to accept disruption to their customary routine, to travel many miles often in the company of strange dogs, to mix with strange dogs at the show, to be handled sometimes very unceremoniously by strange people, and to give off all the while an air of quiet confidence and enjoyment which enables them to look their best.

A dog which doesn't travel well, cannot mix with other dogs or will not be handled by strangers has no future as a show dog. A dog which is quarrelsome or aggressive is not only exposed to the risk of being banned from shows, but also to having its registration cancelled and so its ability to produce registered offspring terminated.

Pat dogs can also be show dogs. (Photo. E. Jackson)

Preparation

The early training which is intended to produce a show dog is no different from that appropriate to any other puppy. Scrupulous attention to socializing the dog and to producing a confident but sociable and even-tempered animal is required as much for companions and workers as for show dogs. Some exhibitors begin training as early as three weeks, the basics being to stand happily on a table and undergo a thorough examination, to walk smartly on a loose lead, to turn and return to a given place, and to stop and stand smartly.

Some breeds place great emphasis on barbering as the basis for presentation. However, Border Terriers are not one of these, and the first aim in preparing a Border for show is to produce an animal which is clean, fit, well muscled and sound. This cannot be achieved without a great deal of hard, though enjoyable, work on the part of both owner and dog. Attention to cleanliness is important. Few judges are going to be much impressed by a dog from which arises the easily identified stench of neglect and which leaves his/her hands greasy after examination. A clean coat and pelt, neatly clipped nails, clean teeth, bright, clean eyes and clean ears are all part and parcel of having a well cared-for dog.

In the rough.

Coats, perhaps, have the greatest superficial effect on appearance and are certainly a favourite subject for discussion when Border folk get together, but they are not created by skilled trimming or by tonsorial expertise: they are created by breeding and feeding. Unfortunately, skill with a knife and scissors can help to disguise a poor coat, and make a semblance of a silk purse out of a sow's ear that will deceive some judges. Nevertheless, while the phrase 'essentially a working terrier' remains in the Breed Standard and has any meaning, coats on Border Terriers should be double, weather-resistant, lasting and natural.

The implements needed to prepare a Border Terrier for the show ring are essentially scissors, to trim the feet; clippers, for the nails; a comb or terrier pad, for finishing touches; and most important of all, the finger and thumb. Dead coat and long hair are removed, a few at a time, simply by plucking with finger and thumb. This also applies to the topknot; ear fringes; and to hair in the ears, down the neck, on the rear of the legs, on the keel and tuck-up, and on the underside of the tail. Initially this takes time, but no great skill is required to turn a hairy Border Terrier into a very presentable creature. The important thing to remember is that Border Terriers must have a good undercoat and a harsh, tweedy top coat: the use of stripping knives will destroy the undercoat and leave the top coat smooth and silky, not at all what is required by anyone who truly appreciates the breed.

There is, nowadays, a regrettable tendency for good dogs to be taken to shows when they are not in the best condition. They may fool bad judges or make a fool of weak ones, but they do neither themselves nor their owners any credit. Exhibitors who show dogs which have no more coat than is to be found on a side of bacon, or conversely, with coat down to their knees; bitches heavy in whelp; or dogs grossly fat or otherwise out of condition, should not feel aggrieved if they are placed below dogs that look their best.

Exhibitors should get to the show in good time to acquaint themselves with the arrangements, for their dog to become acclimatized to the environment, and – if they are not involved in the first classes to be judged, usually for puppy dogs – to familiarize themselves with the procedure adopted by the judge. The dog should be given an opportunity to empty himself, to have a small drink and perhaps even a small feed, after which he should be encouraged to rest quietly until the time comes for him to enter the ring. Some shows provide benches for exhibits, some provide accommodation for caged dogs, and this includes many which provide benches, too. If dogs are accustomed to being caged they can be transported in greater safety, and at the show will be more secure and better able to rest. They will then enter the ring fresh and alert, ready to do their best.

On the table waiting for the judge.

The aim of an exhibitor is to ensure that the judge is aware of the dog's virtues and is kept in ignorance of its faults, and to achieve this aim without in any way interfering with other exhibits or exhibitors. Showing calls for skills which may not be apparent to the newcomer, but close observation and attendance at ring training classes will quickly turn even complete rawness into competence.

The trophy table.

Championship Status

In Britain a dog must win three Challenge Certificates, the third being won after it has passed its first birthday, under three different judges before it can claim the title of champion. In 1996 there were just twenty-eight Challenge Certificates for Border Terriers allocated to each sex. In theory, Championship status remains constant in any particular country, though it must differ from one to another, if only because of the different systems employed. Theory and practice, however, do not always coincide.

The 'good' old days.

For example in 1980 a total of 2,098 Border Terriers were entered at the twenty-nine British shows which then had CCs on offer for the breed. The highest entry was at the Southern Border Terrier Club Championship Show, with 149 dogs entered, and the lowest was at the Blackpool Championship Show where there were fifty-two dogs. In 1980 an average of 72.34 dogs competed for each set of CCs available in the breed.

By 1990 the picture had changed dramatically, when 4,086 dogs competed for thirty-three sets of CCs. The lowest number of dogs, sixty-two, was at the Paignton Championship Show, and the highest, 277, was once again at the Southern Border Terrier Club Championship Show. In 1990 an average of 123.8 dogs competed for each set of CCs available to the breed.

Even without taking other factors into account – the quality of the dogs competing, and the competence and integrity of judges, for example – it is apparent that the value of Challenge Certificates did not remain constant throughout the decade.

It is far harder for a dog – and certainly much harder for a Border

*tos., **E. Bell**, *Bolton, Amble.*
WINNING BORDER TERRIERS AT ALWINTON BORDER SHEPHERDS' SHOW.

The Alwinton Border Shepherd's Show.

Terrier – to become a champion in Britain than anywhere else in the world. There are several reasons for this. One is that far more Border Terriers compete at British Championship Shows than elsewhere. Furthermore, Britain has only twenty-eight shows at which Challenge Certificates are on offer to Border Terriers; some other countries have far more shows and far fewer entries.

Another reason is that in many countries the rules require that dogs which have become champions no longer compete with aspiring champions; the path to Championship status is thus eased by the removal of dogs which have already achieved that status. In Britain, however, existing champions continue to compete, sometimes remorselessly, for Challange Certificates, and their presence in the ring ensures that competition is kept at the highest possible level.

Britain has yet another practice which tends to ensure testing competition: the majority of British Championship Show judges are themselves people who have achieved appreciable success in the breed, and their knowledge is indisputable. Elsewhere it is rare, even unknown, for judges with practical experience of the breed to judge it. Efforts to compensate for this lack of practical experience by means of examinations appear to have only limited success.

A rare double. (Photo. Alan Walker.)

The first Championship Show, as far as the breed is concerned, took place at Carlisle and was judged, appropriately enough, by Simon Dodd; his dog CC winner was Tinker, his bitch was Liddesdale Bess. Tinker was a yearling dog bred by Mr W. Harrison by Gyp, whose name was subsequently changed to North Tyne Gyp, himself bred by N. Cockrane; he was by Geoff out of Wannie of Tynedale. Tinker was out of Daisy, herself bred by Willie Barton, and was by Venter out of his homebred Venus. Liddesdale Bess had been born in August 1917 and so was more mature than the dog. She was bred by James Davidson, and was by Liddesdale Nailer out of Davidson's homebred but unregistered Pearl, Nailer having been bred by Willie Barton, whose name frequently recurs as an important breeder during the early years of the Border Terrier's career as a show dog.

Nowadays the majority of regular exhibitors regard club shows as the competitive and social high points in the show calendar. This high regard is easily understood. The club Championship Shows, in particular, attract far higher entries than any other show, and these usually include a greater number of champions and CC winners than any other, too. The judges are appointed by their peers and are invariably people whose opinion commands respect in the breed. The importance which is nowadays attached to these shows contrasts sharply with the fact that no club Championship Shows existed prior to World War II;

119

it was only in 1946, when shows resumed after the interregnum caused by the war, that the Kennel Club decided to award Championship status to both the Border Terrier Club and the Southern Border Terrier Club.

Club Shows

The Border Terrier Club has held its annual Championship Show ever since. Its first show was judged by John Renton, who chose Mr and Mrs Adam Forster's wheaten Fire Fighter and Bladnoch Spaewife as his CC winners. The Southern Border Terrier Club's 1946 show was also unusual in that the dogs were judged by the well known Scottish all-rounder Jimmy Garrow, and the bitches by W. Lewis Renwick, the steward for both being Lionel Hamilton Renwick, now a respected Championship Show judge of the breed. The dog CC winner was Norman Fielden's Vanda Daredevil, a dog who had an eye put out while more demandingly employed, but who nevertheless continued on his winning ways. The bitch winner was Phyllis Mulcaster's home-bred Portholme Mab.

Willie Hancock's Ch. Vanda Daredevil.

The Club held another Championship Show in 1947, but then not again until 1952. Another was held in 1953, after which the Club relinquished its Championship status until 1980; in this year Jean Jackson, after running a number of successful open shows for the Club, took charge of the first of the series of Southern Club Championship Shows held at Cheltenham Racecourse – this fixture has now grown into the biggest gathering of Border Terriers and their admirers anywhere in the world.

In 1986 the show became the first in the breed to attract more than 200 dogs. John Creed judged, and the dog CC was won by Stewart MacPherson and Ted Hutchinson's Brannigan of Brumberhill, and the bitch CC by Betty Judge's Plushcourt on Target. In 1990 Brian Staveley found that he had an even more demanding task when he was faced with 277 dogs. At the end of the day the winners were Valmyre Magician of Dandyhow and Jean and Frank Jackson's Ch. Stonekite Soft Soap by Clipstone.

The Yorkshire, Lancashire and Cheshire Border Terrier Club achieved Championship status in 1962. Its first show was judged by Phyllis Mulcaster whose winners were John Renton's and Ted Harper's Ch. Barnikin and Robert Hall's Browside Rip of Deerstone. In 1991 the winners at a record Club show with 236 dogs, judged by Anne Roslin Williams, were Dave and Trak Fryer's Ch. Dandyhow April Fool and Jean and Frank Jackson's Ch. Stonekite Charisma by Clipstone.

The Northern Border Terrier Club joined the band in 1973 when Mary Roslin Williams was invited to judge the inaugural event. Her winners were Bertha Sullivan's Ch. Dandyhow Shady Knight and Edna Garnett's Rhosmerholme Capacious. In 1989 the show received its highest total of dogs when Bob Williams judged 198 dogs and 241 entries.

In 1981 the four clubs combined, each acting as host in turn, to run a Joint Clubs' Championship Show. The event proved to be very popular and got off to an excellent and appropriate start when Mrs Bertha Sullivan made an all-too-rare appearance in the centre of the ring. Perhaps her reluctance to judge contributed to the fact that she has never been invited to judge at Cruft's the breed to which she has contributed so much, and in which she has achieved such outstanding success. Cruft's reputation is thereby diminished. Mrs Sullivan had 121 dogs to judge. The CC winners were Tez and Genna Tuck's Lyddington Let's Go and Wilf Wrigley's Duttonlea Steel Blue. In 1988 Bob Williams judged a record number of dogs for the show, 223, from which Milnethorpe Noble Sportsman at Bretcar and Kathie Wilkinson's Otterkin Tapestry emerged as the CC winners. Sadly the

Kennel Club has since decided to strike this very popular show from the calendar to make way for less well supported events.

Next to enter the lists was the Scottish Border Terrier Club whose inaugural show was judged by Jean Jackson in 1985. The CCs were won by two blue and tans, Gordon Knight's Ch. Sundalgo Slate Blue and Frank Wildman and John Bainbridge's Ch. Ragsdale Blue Covert. This first show attracted 128 dogs, but in 1994, when Brian Baxter was the judge, the muster had grown to 177 dogs and 247 entries with Dave and Trak Fryer's Irton First Footer and Kate Irving's Dandyhow Cleopatra taking the honours.

In 1989 the Midland Border Terrier Club became the sixth breed club to hold a Championship Show, the Club President, Ted Hutchinson, judging the first event with 168 dogs. The winners at this inaugural fixture were Steve Dean's Tyrian Bluebeard and Kathie Wilkinson's Ch. Otterkin Singin' the Blues. In 1992, when Elspeth Jackson judged the show, there were 217 dogs and 276 entries, from which Dave and Trak Fryer's veteran Ch. Dandyhow April Fool and Kath Wilkinson's Otterkin Blue Note emerged as the principal winners.

Judging

There are certain exhibitors who still have some way to go before they cease to be novices who entertain ambitions to judge: little do they realize that every judge is subjected to the assessment of a very critical and very knowledgeable ringside. One very confident novice was once unwise enough to boast that she found Border Terriers very easy to judge – she was told, in no uncertain terms, that she would find them harder to judge when she knew more about them.

In Britain, all that is needed to become a judge is an invitation. However, only someone very foolish would allow personal ambition to over-ride prudence and good sense and enter the ring without knowing what exhibitors expect. The pressures to which all judges are subject may not always be apparent – though sometimes they are obvious for all to see.

Exhibitors do not come forward purely to provide judges with the opportunity to exercise their egos or their prejudices: on the contrary, judges should provide a service to exhibitors. It is one which exhibitors pay for, in that simply by entering a class they provide the judge with an opportunity which would not otherwise exist. The judge should be grateful for this, and in return exhibitors have the right to expect judges to be competent, honest, efficient, thorough, courteous, knowl-edgeable and unprejudiced. If he fails in any of these respects, the judge should, at the least, not expect exhibitors to reappear when he next judges, he might also expect future appointments to be less easy to come by, and finally he should not be surprised if complaints about his behaviour are placed before the Kennel Club.

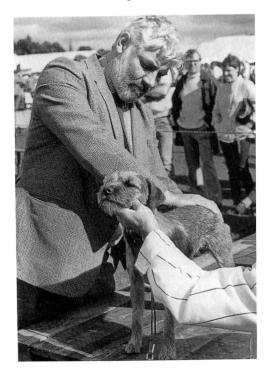

A thorough examination.

Individuals who are able ro resist the temptation to become judges are rare, although sometimes the temptation comes second to a fear of the isolation and the responsibility which are to be found in the centre of a ring. Less often they stem from an honest recognition of limita-tions. The late Captain Henry d'O Vigne was for many years chairman of the Southern Border Terrier Club; his attitude to committee deci-sions was somewhat like the Duke of Wellington's who, on becoming Prime Minister, told his cabinet what they had to decide and was then surprised that they wanted to stay on and discuss the issue. No club has ever had a better or more honest chairman than Henry Vigne. However, he never judged under KC rules. Those who valued his opinion decided that perhaps this was because Henry had only one eye, though through the remaining eye he saw more, especially about Border Terriers, than most do with two good eyes. We were delegated to ask Henry to judge. Our advances were accepted with typical courtesy and good humour but were firmly rejected. Our subsequent efforts to change his mind at least evoked the reason for his attitude:

'I have,' said Henry, 'a well developed critical sense but no comparative sense, and I don't believe that I would be a good judge.'

And that was that. What a pity Henry's self-knowledge and integrity is not more widespread. One world-famous judge was criticised by someone who knew him very well indeed:

'He has only one fault as a judge, he can't recognize quality.' Perhaps a couple of the stories which bad judges give rise to will help illustrate what a bad judge must endure:

'I had a strange dream last night. I dreamt that I had died and gone to Heaven.'

'What was it like?'

'Super! It was an enormous dog show and I had the most marvellous entry judge.'

'What a coincidence, I had a dream very like that except that I went to Hell.'

'Oh dear, what was it like?'

'It was absolutely terrible; *you* were judging!'

On another occasion a ringside judge offered his unsought opinion:

'If I had judged this show I certainly wouldn't have placed your dog.'

'If you had been judging this show, my dog wouldn't have been entered.'

Some judges are needlessly rough when they examine a dog. Whether this roughness stems from a misplaced belief that working terriers should be handled harshly, from a self-defeating intention to test their temperament by provoking them into retaliation, from a malicious intention to unnerve them or simply from incompetence, it is difficult to say. What *is* certain, however, is that rough handling is not only unnecessary, it is not the best way of gaining information about a particular dog. It is also certain that a reputation for rough handling will deny a judge the opportunity to handle dogs whose owners object to such pointless torment.

Judges would do well to remember that while their task is to deliver an opinion about the dogs before them, they are also exposing themselves to judgement, and frequently the delivery of a stongly adverse opinion, from all those at the ringside. Some years ago a judge found

Jean Jackson judging in 1976.

himself confronted by a bitch puppy class containing twenty-three exhibits. He judged them with apparent efficiency, and the occasion would not have excited notice had he not subsequently offered a hostage to fortune by writing in his critique that though the class was exceptionally large it contained nothing of outstanding merit. In fact it contained no fewer than five bitches which went on to gain their titles, two of which were outstanding in their time and both of which received CCs from the disappointed judge.

On another occasion, after what seemed an interminable length of time during which ringsiders had become increasingly bored and restless at the judge's apparent reluctance to make decisions, the time came from him to judge the four winning puppies in order to award Best Puppy in Show. All four had won their respective classes, and all four were again paraded before the self-same judge – who reacted as though he had never seen them before! Each was again examined, moved, deliberated over, and time ticked slowly by until at last he moved hesitantly towards his chosen winner. And after all these painful deliberations he contrived to select the one puppy among the four which would not become a champion. Had he made the same error speedily and efficiently it might have been less memorable!

Ambitious judges often seem to feel that progress in their chosen trade will be enhanced if they dress in a memorable manner. James

Garrow used to wear a large black fedora, George Leatt wore a thick tweed plus-four suit – even in the hottest weather, Herbert Essam sported a plastic orchid buttonhole, Harry Glover carried a yellow duster. Ronnie Irving used to have a red handkerchief in his top pocket, but dropped the affectation when he found that all his exhibitors were also wearing a red handkerchief in their top pockets!

Other Competitive Activities

Junior Handling
by Elspeth Jackson

Having grown up in a household which, in my lifetime, has never been without several Border Terriers, I have been showing dogs almost since I could walk. In those not very distant days junior handling competitions were taken seriously only by the youngsters who competed in them. The judges chosen to assess our ability to handle dogs were often themselves atrocious handlers. There was no pattern set for competition, no standard basis for assessment and, too often, no recognition that young competitors were doing their best and had a right to have their efforts taken seriously.

Handlers start young.

126

Border terriers are good with children who are good with Border terriers. (Photo. J. Jackson.)

Things have changed. Nowadays a successful competitor in junior handling competitions can expect to be judged by people who have proved their ability to handle dogs in the ring. The reward is not a condescending pat on the head and a bar of chocolate, but an opportunity to take part in similar competitions in various parts of the world.

Junior handling has come of age, and although in the process it may have lost some of its former innocence, it has certainly become an integral part of the international world of dog shows.

Mini Agility
by Betty Orrin

Mini agility has become very popular over the last few years. Class entries have increased, and also the number of classes scheduled at shows, although many still do not run mini classes which are the ones appropriate to Border Terriers. In many ways, mini agility is more interesting to watch than standard height agility, as there is a greater spectrum of breeds seen. There are several Borders entering now.

In order to be able to compete in mini agility, only dogs 15in (38cm) and under in height are allowed to enter. Borders should be ideal for this sport as they are racy and light on their feet, have normal body dimensions, and no known breed problems. It is important to keep it fun for them, as Borders have a low boredom threshold. None of the equipment should present a problem to Borders, even the 'A' frame, since their length of leg is sufficient to make scaling it easy (some other mini breeds often have trouble with this piece of equipment especially initially).

Agility competition.

Whilst it is possible to teach the dog using home-made equipment, it is advisable to join one of the many agility clubs. These have all the equipment you will need, and the expertise to ensure the initial training ends with your dog keen and happy to do more. Most of the good clubs will also teach you to handle the dog on both sides – essential to take short cuts if you are not as agile as your dog!

It is an addictive sport, with people travelling miles in order to spend a few seconds running round a ring! As there are still few mini people about, it is easy to make good and lasting friendships. The Agility Club runs courses for instructors and competitors.

Working Trials

In the United States and in those countries under the jurisdiction of the Fédération Cynologique Internationale, arrangements exist for testing the working ability of Border Terriers. In the United States the tests were primarily designed with Border Terriers in mind, whereas the FCIs tests were originally intended for Dachshunds.

*A seasoned campaigner
relaxes at a show.*

It is entirely likely that similar tests may eventually be introduced
into Britain, but as yet those which do exist are privately organized.

Obedience

Anyone looking for a dog capable of being trained to be instantly
obedient and to compete at the highest level in obedience trials would
not first think of getting a Border Terrier. Nevertheless, some owners
have managed to overcome the breed's customary independence
sufficiently to acquit themselves well in novice obedience competitions.

Flyball

A competitive activity which has only relatively recently crossed
the Atlantic, flyball exploits the enjoyment which dogs derive from
chasing, catching and retrieving flying objects.

8

Top Dogs and Companions

Leading Kennels

Several volumes would be needed to do anything like justice to all the breeders and owners who, over many years, have contributed to the development of the Border Terrier. That particular luxury is not available, and so some process of selection – that word again rears its head! – becomes necessary. It is not uncommon for Border Terrier owners to make their first show dog into a champion. Good, honourable judges assess *dogs*, and not people or their reputations, whether good or bad, and a good dog, well conditioned, trained and presented will be recognized by any knowledgeable and honest judge, even though it is in the hands of a novice handler.

Mr and Mrs Adam Forster's Ch. Future Fame.

Any breeder may, whether by good fortune or good management, produce a dog which becomes a champion. The list is already long and it grows year by year, and it isn't possible to give each its undoubted due. To date there have been just over five hundred British champions, a far smaller number than in countries where competition is less stringent but where the process of becoming a champion is less demanding.

Kennels which, over the years, produce a succession of champions might reasonably be said to rely on something other than good fortune. Such is the level of competition and the difficulty of becoming a champion that in Britain during the last seventy-five years only seven kennels have produced ten or more British champions. Only two, Bertha and Kate Irving's Dandyhow and Jean, Elspeth and Frank Jackson's Clipstone, have produced more than twenty. Then come Peter and Maureen Thompson's Thoraldbys and Anne Roslin Williams' Manserghs each with eighteen. Even so, let us be the first to acknowledge that a large number of champions doesn't count for everything: to have bred Ch. Dandyhow Shady Knight, Ch. Billy Boy, Dandyhow Brussel Sprout, Ch. Future Fame, Ch. Thoraldby Tiptoes, Ch. Brannigan of Brumberhill or Ch. Step Ahead is a perfectly adequate justification for pride. But it must still be accepted that the kennels which exert a major influence on the breed are those which produce a number of champions over an appreciable period of time.

David Black's advertisement for his Tweedside kennel.

The first **Tweedside Red** Border Terrier champion was Ch. Tweedside Red Type (1920), and the last of the kennel's eight champions was Ch. Tweedside Red Glamorous (1949), though the kennel continued to produce CC winners until the mid-1950s. Its major influence was exerted through Tweedside Red Kingpin who, though not himself a champion, was the sire of five champions, Ch. Rab Roy (1958), Ch. Brieryhill Gertrude, Ch. Happy Day, Ch. Barnikin and Ch. Bright Light, the last four of which were all born in 1959.

Wattie Irving's first champion was Ch. Station Masher (1924), the last Ch. Bright Light (1959). Among the champions produced in the meanwhile was Ch. Rising Light (1945), whose unusually long career as a CC winner continued from 1946 to 1951. Wattie Irving's influence over the breed during the early years after recognition, and again during the difficult post-war period, was considerable but it was perhaps through his family that he exerted the greatest influence. He was the father of Andrew, a Championship Show judge, and father-in-law of Mervyn Gaddes, also a Championship Show judge, grandfather of Grace Gaddes, owner of Ch. Hornpiece Salvia (1950) and Ch. Gay Gordon (1962), and of Ronnie, who owned and bred champions in his own right, including the double CC winners, litter-brother and sister, Ch. South – properly pronounced 'Sooth' – Box (1976) and Ch. Din Merry (1976), before marrying Kate Sullivan and becoming pontiff to the Dandyhow kennel.

Photo., Thos. Fall.
MR. J. T. RENTON'S CH. HAPPY MOOD.

Mr J.T. Renton's Ch. Happy Mood. (Photo. Thomas Fall.)

*Two of the breed's 'greats',
John Renton with Ch. Happy
Day. (Photo. Jean Jackson.)*

   John Renton, who never found it necessary to treat himself to the
luxury of a kennel affix, was the first to produce more than ten champions. Starting with Ch. Todhunter (1930), he quietly got on with the
job of producing a succession of champions, and they included some
outstanding Border Terriers. The spectacular Ch. Happy Day (1959) by
Tweedside Red Kingpin out of Happy Morn, owned and bred by John
Renton, remains firmly in the mind's eye, as do the home-bred and
owned Ch. Handy Andy (1965) by Ch. Hawkesburn Beaver out of
Border Queen. Handy Andy's full sister Ch. Hawkesburn Happy
Returns (1966), made up in the ownership of Felicity Marchant,
brought the kennel's long and unrivalled career to an end.

HALLBOURNE BADGER
by Aldham Joker ex Cronas Birkie
Bred by Mr. S. Kealey

Kally Twist's advertisement.

The first champion for Kally Twist's **Hallbourne** kennel was Ch. Wedale Jock (1934), and the second was the important sire Ch. Aldham Joker (1937), the father of seven champions and whose influence was extended by his son Ch. Hallbourne Badger (1950). The kennel's last champion was Ch. Hallbourne Constancy (1954).

Lady Marjory Russell's **Swallowfield** kennel was another which sustained its success over many years. Beginning with Ch. Finchale Lass (1937) and ending with Ch. Dandyhow Sandpiper (1968) (litter-brother to Ch. Dandyhow Shady Knight), the kennel in the meantime produced a succession of champions which included Ch. Swallowfield Garry, a dog ahead of his time. Lady Russell's husband had connections with the Great Western Railway, and this provided a unique opportunity to have a steam engine carry her affix.

Ch. Leatty Lace (1947), by Bladnoch Brock of Deerstone out of Leatty Sadie and bred by A. Pethybridge, launched the **Leatty** kennel's career in the ownership of the well known allrounder George Leatt, who to date has judged the breed more often at Championship Shows than any other judge. All the subsequent Leatty Border Terrier champions were registered in the ownership of Phyllis Leatt; she produced a succession of eleven champions, the last being Ch. Leatty Felldyke Gorse (1965), bred by John Harrison, by Ch. Joytime out of Felldyke Bracken. Gorse ended his show career in the hands of Norman Cowgill.

Robert Hall's **Deerstone** kennel's first association with a champion was via Barbara Holmes' Ch. Portholme Marthe of Deerstone (1946) by Ch. Aldham Joker out of Portholme Ruby. She was bred by A. Sanson and thus was neither bred nor owned by – at least during her

CALLUM
(Ch. Fox Lair—Dipley Dinah)

SWALLOWFIELD GARRY
(Ch. Aldham Joker—Swallowfield Solo)

The Swallowfield kennel's Callum and Swallowfield Garry, taken from Swallowfield's advertisement in Our Dogs, Christmas 1947.

Photo.. E. Guy, Reading.
SWALLOWFIELD SHINDY

The first ever English and Continental International Champion of the Breed

Int Ch. Golden Imperialist, the first ever English and Continental International Champion of the Breed.

show career – either of the kennels whose affix she carried. Its dogs always superbly presented, the Deerstone kennels was to produce, among others, the renowned home-bred Ch. Deerstone Destiny (1955) and Ch. Deerstone Douglas (1962), whose short show and stud career was a loss to the breed. The kennel's last champion may well have been

WHARFHOLM Kennels
Mrs. B. S. T. HOLMES
INGS LANE, GUISELEY, NR. LEEDS

CHAMPION DEERSTONE DRIVER

Telephone
Guiseley 190

Station
L. M. S.
Guiseley

AT the club show, where I judged over 50 Borders, I made **Ch. Deerstone Driver** best of breed, and gave him the c.c. in dogs; he stood streets away, but he had to contend with at least three outstanding bitches. Very few dogs of any terrier breed stand so near to the standard as Driver. Driver can sire good ones, for his daughter, **Wharfholm Winnie** was a good Winner at this show. She only needs time and a litter, to become contender for top honours. Winnie has had much success. She is out of Portholme Marthe of Deerstone, who like Driver has won two c.c.s and between them they have collected a record number of reserve c.c.s under the most able of Border Terrier judges. **Deer**stone **Dancer** is another that has done great things, at all sorts of shows, and she has stood at, or near, the top in breed as well as in A.V. classes.

At Ings Lane, the Borders are kept in ideal country conditions, with ample exercising space and they have a hardy outdoor life.

Mrs. Holmes sometimes has puppies for sale. **Deerstone Driver**, red grizzle.—Winner of c.c. and best of breed, Manchester, 1951, c.c. and best of breed, and special for best otter head. Met. and Essex, Olympia, 1951; reserve c.c., Altrincham and Leicester, 1950, Cheltenham and Richmond 1951; very many wins at open shows; runner-up, B.I.S., Honley. Proved sire of great

otter headed stock. Stud Fee 3 gns. and return carriage. Driver may be inspected at anytime. **Portholme Marthe of Deerstone.**—Winner of c.c. and best of breed, Bournemouth 1951; c.c. Richmond, 1951; reserve c.c. at nine other shows; reserve bitch c.c. at the L.K.A.; best bitch in show, all breeds, Northallerton, 1951; regular winner in A.V. classes.

Deerstone Dancer. –Best bitch in show, Ilkley, 1951; winner at ch. open and other shows. **Wharfholm Winnie,** best puppy bitch, at the Border Club ch. show, Carlisle, 1951, then under 8 months of age, a very consistent winner since then.

H. G. Sanders.

WHARFHOLM WINNIE

PORTHOLME MARTHE OF DEERSTONE

Barbara Holmes' advertisement in Our Dogs, Christmas 1951.

its best bitch: Ch. Deerstone Falcliff Ramona (1967) was bred by Ellis Mawson and originally owned by Mrs Fairly, although it was Robert Hall who piloted her to her well deserved title.

The first two champions associated with Barbara Holmes **Wharfholm** kennel were Ch. Portholme Marthe of Deerstone (1946) and Ch. Deerstone Driver (1947), the young dog reaching its title before its slightly older kennel-mate. The kennel's peak was perhaps reached with Ch. Wharfholm Warrant (1966), the sire of seven champions including Ch Wharfholm Wonderlad (1977), who closed this particular chapter in the breed's history.

It is difficult to overestimate the corporate influence which certain Yorkshire-based kennels were to have on the breed when circumstances made an unusual degree of co-operation necessary: Arthur Duxbury's **Ribbleside**, Robert Hall's Deerstone, Barbara Holmes Wharfholm, Phylis Leatt's Leatty and, somewhat later on the scene, Arthur Beardwood's **Chevinor**, Edna Garnett's **Rhosmerholme**, Marsden's **Braestone**, Ellis Mawson's **Falcliff**, Harry Walker's **Cravendale** and Wilf Wrigley's **Duttonlea**.

Adam Forster's kennel was another of those which scorned the use of an affix, though three of the kennel's five champions – Ch. Future Fame (1948), Ch. First Footer (1949), and Ch. Fine Features (1950) – as well as other influential dogs produced by the kennel, made use of the repeated capital 'F' in their names. The kennel's first champion was Ch. Winnie (1919), and its last the Ch. Fine Features (1950), one of the eight champions sired by the kennel's most influential dog Ch. Future Fame (1948).

Bobby and Edna Benson's first champion was Ch. Joytime (1953), but the **Daletyne** affix exerted its main influence through Daletyne Rory, the sire of four champions, Ch. Highland Gyp (1964), Ch. Daletyne Dundrum (1964), Ch. Daletyne Batchelor (1964) and Ch. Daletyne Decora (1965), in addition to which he produced three CC winners. The kennel crammed a great deal of success into a few years.

Walter Gardner's **Maxton** affix burned brightly but for a relatively short time, from Ch. Maxton Mannequin (1954) to Ch. Maxton Monarch (1963), but in that short time the kennel produced seven champions, perhaps the most significant of which was Ch. Maxton Matchless (1956), who was himself the sire of three champions.

Ch. **Eignwye** Enchantress (1957) was the first champion bred and owned by Bob Williams. The kennel, now in retirement, went on to produce four more champions, the last being Ch. Eignwye Wheatear (1975).

Madelene Aspinwall's **Farmway** kennel was founded on Ch. Covington Dove (1957), a daughter of Ch. Carahall Cornet, from Donald Goodsir's **Carahall** kennel. It continued with the long-lasting Ch. Farmway Red Robin (1962), and its most recent champion, Ch. Brindon Bravado of Farmway (1988), continued the kennel's winning ways.

The **Mansergh** affix is one of the breed's aristocrats supported by a small kennel dedicated to producing top quality Border Terriers. After over forty years the kennel has bred about 150 puppies. It was first owned by Mary Roslin Williams, to whom must go the credit for the success of Ch. Mansergh Wharfholm Wistful (1958), and then by Mary's daughter, Anne Roslin Williams, and is one of the most successful in the breed having produced, among a long line of champions, Ch. Mansergh Pearl Diver (1978) and Ch. Mansergh Toggle, respectively the sire and dam of three champions.

Kate Irving's Ch. Dandyhow Cleopatra.

Bertha Sullivan's **Dandyhow** affix burst onto the championship scene with Ch. Dandyhow Suntan (1961) and Ch. Dandyhow Sultana (1961). Throughout the 1960s, 1970s, 1980s and 1990s the kennel has produced champion after champion: it now has twenty-seven to its credit, the most recent being Kate Irving's Ch. Dandyhow Bright Sparkle (1994). Mention of some of·its outstanding dogs are sprinkled throughout this section, but it would take more than one chapter to provide a proper appreciation of the influence which this kennel has exerted over the breed for almost four decades. The record speaks for itself.

Ch **Hawkesburn** Beaver (1963) was the first champion in Felicity Marchant's kennel which went on to produce some very typical bitches including Ch. Hawkesburn Happy Returns (1966), Ch. Hawkesburn Nutmeg (1970) and Ch. Hawkesburn Spindle (1973).

The first champion owned by **Ronnie Irving**, who followed the family tradition of scorning the use of an affix, was Ch. Bounty Tanner (1965), bred by Tom Newall, mine host at the Bounty Inn. Tanner sired Ch. Arnton Fell (1969). Ch. Llanishen Penelope (1971) became the kennel's next champion, and was followed by the litter-brother and sister Chs South Box and Din Merry (1976).

In 1965, Dorothy Miller bred Ch. **Foxhill** Fusilier and until 1976 when Ch. Foxhill Fantastic was born this small kennel produced a succession of outstanding bitch champions, including the two Shady Knight daughters, Feonix (1970) and Fidelity (1972).

Ch. Oxcroft Vixen (1966) was the first champion to carry Jack Price's **Oxcroft** affix. She was followed by Ch. Oxcroft Moonmagic (1969), Ch. Oxcroft Pearl of Mansergh (1973), Ch. Oxcroft Rocker (1978), Ch. Oxcroft Tally (1980) and the appropriately named Ch. Oxcroft Rogue (1991).

Gilbert Walker's **Workmore** kennel was one of several with a strong working background. Its first champion was Ch. Workmore Bracken (1968), followed by the exceptionally typey Ch. Workmore Rascal (1973) and the influential sire Ch. Workmore Waggoner (1973).

Wilf Wrigley's **Duttonlea** affix is now in retirement, but from the home-bred Ch. Duttonlea Mr Softy (1968) until the litter brother and sister Ch. Duttonlea Suntan of Dandyhow (1980), and the dam of four champions Ch. Steel Blue produced several champions.

Jean, Elspeth and Frank Jackson's **Clipstone** kennel's first champion was Ch. Clipstone Hanleycastle Bramble (1969), bred by Roger Clements. The kennel was then fortunate to acquire a Brussel Sprout daughter whose first litter contained Ch. Clipstone Carrots 1970 and Ch. Clipstone Guardsman (1970). Carrots then produced Ch. Clipstone Cetchup (1973) who won his first CC at seven months and had collected three before his puppy career came to an end. His blue-and-tan litter brother Corsican won two CCs before exchanging a show career for life in a bishop's palace. Int. Ch. Bombax Xavier (1975) joined the kennel from Gunnar and Carl Gunnar Stafberg's Swedish **Bombax** kennel to become the first, and as yet the only, British Border Terrier champion born outside these islands. Ch. Clipstone Cumin (1982) had the good fortune to produce, in his proving litter, the first two of his six champion offspring, Ch. Bannerdown Boomerang (1983) and Ch. Bannerdown Cavalier (1983) for Pam Creed's Bannerdown kennel. The kennel's most recent champion, Ch. Starcyl Penny Red Clipstone (1993), bred by Rita MacCrystal, was its twenty-first British champion.

Dennis Wiseman's **Llanishen** affix is one of those which is rooted in work but which also produced a succession of show champions. The first was Ch. Llanishen Illse of Clipstone (1970), and the most recent, Ch. Llanishen Red Eagle (1979).

The father and daughter partnership of Harry and Jean Singh bred their first champion, Ch. **Vandamere's** Band of Gold in 1970, and went on to produce more home-bred champions including Ch. Vandamere's Burnished Gold (1973) and Ch. Vandamere's Daybreak (1974), culminating in Ch. Vandamere's Daylight (1980). Happily family commitments now allow Jean Singh to return to the ring.

The first champion produced by Pete and Maureen Thompson's **Thoraldby** kennel was Ch. Thoraldby Miss Mandy (1972); in due course she became the dam of four champions, an achievement only bettered by two bitches, Ribbleside Morning Dew who bred five champions, and another resident of the Thoraldby kennel, Ch. Loiriston Amber (1981) who not only won twelve CCs but also produced no fewer than six champions.

Ch **Bannerdown** Viscount (1973) was the first Border Terrier champion produced by Pam Creed; he was followed by Ch. Dandyhow Silver Ring (1985) and Ch. Bannerdown Capricorn (1977), the litter brothers Chs Bannerdown Boomerang and Cavalier (1983).

From 1974, when Betty Rumsam bred Ch. **Wilderscot** Beau Bell, this small kennel has produced a steady succession of home-bred champions including Ch. Wilderscot Silver Jubilee (1977), Ch. Wilderscot Morning Star (1978) and, most recently, Ch. Wilderscot Fireworks (1986).

Tag Knight's **Sundalgo** affix was first attached to a home-bred champion in the form of Ch. Sundalgo Salvador (1974), preceded in the kennel by his sire Ch. Oxcroft Moonmagic (1969). In all fairness, Ch. Savinroyd President (1979), made up by Tag Knight after the death of President's owner and breeder Jack Lindley, should be added to the list of the kennel's successes. President was the sire of Ch. Sundalgo Slate Blue (1983).

Ron and Kath Hodgson's **Foxwyn** affix came to the fore with Ch. Thoraldby Yorkshire Lass (1974), and has produced a succession of champions ever since, the most recent of which was Ch. Foxwyn Perfect Nonsense (1993).

Arthur and Elaine Cuthbertson are among that fortunate band of breeders whose first litter contained a champion, Ch. **Ashbrae** Anouska (1975); Ch. Ashbrae Jaffa (1981) and Ch. Ashbrae McNally (1990) have continued the kennel's success.

Brian Baxter's home-bred Ch. Beenaben Brock (1976) marked the kennel's debut in the list of champions. Since then, Ch. Banff of Beenaben (1987) and the litter-mates Ch. Beenaben Bertie and Ch. Beenaben Broidery (1990) have also gained their well deserved crowns.

From Ch. **Brehill** Wayward Lass (1977) Frances Wagstaff has bred bitch champions in successive generations to establish a remarkable record, with Ch. Brehill March Belle (1981), Ch. Brehill April Lass (1984), Ch. Brehill May Belle (1987) and Ch. Brehill Gloster Girl (1991), all of which descend down a single female line.

Mick and Doreen Rushby's **Dormic** affix appeared first on Ch. Grenze Galanthus of Dormic (1979), and has since been proudly carried by Ch. Thoraldby Tiptoes (1982), the sire of eight champions, and his daughter Ch. Cinnamon of Dormic (1985).

Tez and Jenna Tuck's **Nettleby** kennel's first champion was the prolific sire Ch. Lyddington Let's Go (1979), the kennel has since produced the superb Ch. Nettleby Mullein (1984), and Ch. Nettleby Wicked As It Seems (1994).

Stewart McPherson's **Brumberhill** kennel was one of those which achieved success with its first acquisition, Ch. Brumberhill Blue Tansy (1980), and it was to sustain this success by producing a spectacular succession of champions in subsequent years, the most significant of which was certainly the phenomenal winner Ch. Brannigan of Brumberhill. The kennel's most recent champion was Ch. Blue Print at Brumberhill (1994), one of a select band of champions bred by Ted Hutchinson.

Betty Judge established her **Plushcourt** kennel with the declared intention of creating the largest kennel of Border Terriers ever. This ambition was quickly achieved. The kennel also contains a number of other breeds. Its first Border Terrier champion was Ch. Plushcourt on Target (1982), and its most recent was Ch. Rainsbarrow Buzzard at Plushcourt (1991) bred by Dave Westmoreland, and Ch. Blue Owl at Plushcourt (1994) bred by Mr K. Holmes and Mr D. Winsley.

Although Ch. **Rubicon** Rarity (1983) was the first champion to carry Ruth Jordon's cleverly apt affix, the kennel had already been home to Jack Bradley's Ch. Road to Mandalay (1980) and has since produced the home-bred Ch. Rubicon Rarity (1983) and Ch. Rubicon Reserve (1989).

Ch. Dykeside Gordon Ranger.

Ch. Blue Doctor (1982) was the first champion bred and owned by Marjorie Staveley whose **Dykeside** affix has since been carried by Ch. Dykeside Gordon Ranger (1985), both of whom have proved to be influential sires.

Margaret Curtis's appropriately named Ch. First Time **Matamba** (1985) marked the kennel's debut in impressive style; its success has since been continued by the home-bred Ch. Matamba Houdini (1990) and Ch. Matamba Rosemary (1991).

Kathy Wilkinson's litter-mates by Ch. Brannigan of Brumberhill, Ch. **Otterkin** Singin' The Blues (1986) and Ch. Otterkin Tapestry (1986), introduced the kennel to the champions league on a high note; this has been sustained by Ch. Otterkin Blue Note (1991).

Tony Tomlinson's Ch. Lynhay Daz (1987) was the first champion to carry the Lynhay affix which, changed to **Lyndhay**, has since been carried by two more champions: the litter-brothers bred by Jean Gordon, Ch. Without Equal at Lyndhay (1992), and Ch. Dazzle 'em Lyndhay (1992).

Outstanding Dogs

A catalogue of the most successful kennels, success being measured by the number of champions they have produced, inevitably misses some of the outstanding dogs which have been produced by kennels whose success has been more modest. A dog and, equally, a bitch may have an outstanding record in the show ring or as a producer, or it may be one which remains in the memory as something special. To attempt to review these aristocrats of the breed is to venture onto thin ice, since deserving dogs may be missed and those which some regard as less than totally deserving may be included; even so, the attempt must be made.

Tommy Lawrence's homebred Ch. Teri.

Although they may not in themselves have been outstanding dogs, the breed's first two champions, Ch. Teri (1916) and Ch. Liddesdale Bess (1917) certainly deserve a mention. Both won their crowns at the Ayr show in 1921, and both went on to win five Challenge Certificates. Teri was bred by Tommy Lawrence out of unregistered parents, Titlington Jock and Tib; Bess's parents, Nailer and Pearl, were also unregistered. She was bred by Willie Barton who, like Tommy Lawrence, was to have considerable influence on the breed during its formative years as a show dog. Teri won his last CC at the age of seven under Tommy Lawrence, and Bess won hers at the same age under Willie Barton.

Adam Forster's Coquetdale Vic.

The breed's first sire with major significance was Gyp (1917), whose name was later changed to North Tyne Gyp. He was bred by Norman Cockrane, and was by Geoff out of Wannie of Tynedale; he sired a quartet of champions: Ch. Themis (1920), Ch. Grip of Tynedale (1921), Ch. Dandy of Tynedale (1921) and Ch. Daphne (1921).

Mrs David Black, already well known for her Bulldogs, bred Ch. Tweedside Red Tatters (1921) by Ch. Titlington Tatler out of Chip; he was to win a total of nine CCs. Ch. Dandy of Tynedale (1921), by North Tyne Gyp out of Otterburn Lass, bred by John Dodd, also won nine CCs, a total which was not surpassed until Ch. Blister (1932), by Revenge out of Causey Bridget, won his fourteenth CC under John Renton in 1936.

Revenge (1922), bred by Adam Forster (whose 'F.F.' Borders were to become well known), by Buittie out of the tautological Little Midget, sired five champions: Ch. Benton Biddy (1925), Ch. Bladnoch Raiser (1932), Ch. Blister (1929), Ch. Tod Hunter (1930), and Ch. Happy Mood (1930); the last three were out of Causey Bridget, and this established her as the breed's most successful brood-bitch to that date.

There is one dog which, although he had absolutely no influence on the breed, deserves a mention for his unique record: Ch. Southboro' Stray, owned by James Holgate, became a champion in 1927. His breeder, pedigree and even his date of birth are unknown, and if he sired any puppies none appeared in the show ring. He has left no trace on the breed.

Ch. Brimball of Bridge Sollers (1933) was bred and owned by Miss Richmond; she was by Ch. Dinger out of Bunty of Bridge Sollers. She won her fifteenth and last CC in 1936 to establish a record which remained intact for many years. Sadly she does not appear to have been bred from, and so her undoubted quality died with her.

Ch. Aldham Joker (1937), bred by Miss Smither and owned by Kally Twist, was by Ch. Barb Wire out of Country Girl; he was the sire of seven champions: Ch. Boxer Boy (1944), Ch. Swallowfield Garry (1944), Ch. Tweedside Red Biddy (1944), Ch. Portholme Marthe of Deerstone (1946), Ch. Copper of Dipley (1947), Ch. Hallbourne Bracket (1949) and, born when Joker was thirteen years old, Ch. Hallbourne Badger (1950).

Ch. Future Fame (1948) by Fearsome Fellow out of Tombo Squeak went one better and sired Ch. First Footer (1949), Ch. Lucky Purchase (1949), Ch. Fine Features (1950), Ch. Winstonhall Knavesmire Canny Lad (1950), Ch. Alvertune Martin (1950), Ch. Rayndale Ramona (1953), Ch. Maxton Matchless (1956) and Ch. Ranting Roving (1957).

Ch. Billy Boy (1949) was bred by A. Waters and was by Callum out of Misty Dawn. He won three CCs in his own right, but it was as a sire that he excelled: Ch. Redbor Revojet (1952), Ch. Hill Girl (1952), Ch. Braw Boy (1953), Ch. Dipley Dinghy (1955), Ch. Full Toss (1957), Ch. Leatty Billy Bunter (1954), Ch. Silver Sal (1958), Ch. Winstonhall Coundon Tim (1959), Ch. Coundon Trudy (1959) and Ch. Leatty Plough Boy (1959) were the ten champions he produced.

Bertha Sullivan's Dandyhow Brussel Sprout. (Photo. Anne Roslin-Williams.)

This remarkable record was equalled, but not surpassed, by Dandyhow Brussel Sprout (1959). His ten champions were Mary Roslin Williams' Ch. Mansergh Dandyhow Bracken (1961), Ch. Dandyhow Shady Lady (1965), Ch. Dandyhow Sea Shell (1966), Ch. Dandyhow Sweet Biscuit (1967), Ch. Dandyhow Shady Knight (1968), Eva Heslop's Ch. Corburn Ottercap Farm Lassie (1967), Lady Marjory Russell's Ch. Dandyhow Sandpiper (1968), Kitty Walsh's Ch. Thrushgill Dandyhow Silhouette (1968), Harry and Jean Singh's Ch. Vandamere's Band of Gold (1970) and Harold Roper's Ch. Borderbrae Candy (1969).

The tendency, which remains largely intact, for Border Terriers to be retired soon after they had won their title meant that Brimball's record was not threatened, let alone broken, until Bertha Sullivan's Ch. Dandyhow Shady Knight (1968) took the breed by storm to win a total of twenty-four CCs. Even now, almost thirty years after his birth, Shady Knight is regarded by many of those who saw him as the Border Terrier which has come closest to perfection.

Bertha Sullivan's Ch. Dandyhow Shady Knight. (Photo. Anne Roslin-Williams.)

But Shady Knight wasn't just a successful show dog, more importantly he was a successful sire, whose crop of twelve champions still stands as the record. They included Ch. Dandyhow Burnished Silver (1970), Dorothy Miller's Ch. Foxhill Foenix (1970), Ch. Dandyhow Quality Street (1971), Felicity Marchant's Ch. Hawkesburn Nutmeg (1970), Ch. Llannishen Illse of Clipstone (1970) bred by Dennis Wiseman, Dorothy Miller's Ch. Foxhill Fidelity (1972), Jean and Harry Singh's Ch. Vandamere's Burnished Gold (1973), Ch. Dandyhow Spectator (1974), Ch. Oxcroft Pearl of Mansergh (1973) bred by Jack Price, Ch. Dandyhow Nightcap (1975), Pam Creed's Ch. Dandyhow Silver Ring (1975) and Ch. Dandyhow Humbug (1976).

When Harold Jenner bred Ch. Step Ahead (1973), later owned in partnership with Ted Hutchinson, Knight's record came under threat and was eventually surpassed when Step Ahead won his twenty-sixth and final CC in 1976. Ted Hutchinson's handling skills were later employed again to guide Ch. Brannigan of Brumberhill (1984), bred by Harry Deighton and owned by Stewart MacPherson and Ted Hutchinson, to an unprecedented show career during which he collected a total of thirty-one CCs: this established a record which remains intact to this day.

Ch. Biddistone Porcelaine.

As far as bitches are concerned, Brimball's record remained intact until the advent of Ch. Nettleby Mullein (1984); bred and owned by Tez and Jenna Tuck, and by Ch. Lyddington Let's Go out of Blaisdon Souvenir, Mullein collected a total of eighteen CCs. However, this record was beaten in 1996 when Kate Irving's home-bred Ch. Dandyhow Cleopatra (1992) won her nineteenth CC.

Kennels which are well established on a basis of having produced a number of champions are, of course, important to any breed; but so too are those which, having produced their first champion, await the opportunity to go on to greater things. The number of those who, in recent years, have made their first show Border Terrier into a champion, something which we fell a long way short of achieving, effectively gives the lie to the cynical view that owners must become known before their dogs can hope to achieve success. The following are just a few of those which have set their owners on the path to further success:

The Gray family's homebred Ch. Canny Crack of Pontbeck.

Madelene Aspinwall's Ch. Covington Dove (1957), Felicity Marchant's Ch. Hawkesburn Beaver (1963), Dorothy Linley's Ch. Gatehill Coppernob (1966), Catherine Sutton's Ch. Rossut Motcombe Barnbrack (1967), Melanie Lewis's Ch. Eignwye Wheatear (1975), Mrs McAfee's Ch. Braestone Brushwood (1976), Mr and Mrs McKenzie's Ch. Dandyhow Humbug (1976), Joan Gough's Ch. Polydorus Princely Peeler (1977), S. Richardson's Farmway Moneybird (1977), Tez and Jenna Tuck's Ch. Lyddington Let's Go (1979), Mr and Mrs Neville Hackett's Ch. Thistycroft Candlelight (1979), Ron Hillcoat's Ch. Cuilleann Dodger (1980), Andrew Willis's Ch. Oxcroft Tally (1980), Mrs Griffiths' Ch. Bannerdown Boomerang (1983), Eileen Carter's Ch. Polydorus Pop (1983), Carol Mooney's Ch. Thoraldby Tolomeo (1984), Val Myre's Ch. Gem of Valmyre (1984), Margaret Curtis's Ch. First Time Matamba (1985), Dave and Trak Fryer's Ch. Dandyhow April Fool (1985), Frank and Marilyn Danks' Ch. Bushnell's Turtle (1986), Debbie Bass-Pickin's Ch. Basvale Blue Warrior (1986), Miss Coxon's Ch. Borbeck Keneven Electron (1986), Tony Tomlinson's Ch. Lynhay Daz (1987), Mr C. Berry's Ch. Incheril Nitty Gritty (1987), Graeme and

Val Furness' Ch. Quatford Kardinal, by Ch. Durham Red Clipstone, out of Brockhole Blue Ribband at Quatford. (Photo. Val Furness.)

Averil Ramsden's Ch. Orenberg Emperor (1988), Lynda Ward's Ch. Loodal Aristocrat of Roundtown (1988), Mr and Mrs C. Johnson's Ch. Loweldon Bracken (1989), Jane Parker's Ch. Conundrum Anticipation (1990), Miss Barnett's Ch. Brockfox Bracken (1990).

Terriers in Alternative Occupations

Therapy and Assistance

Contact with dogs by people who, for one reason or another, cannot have a dog of their own can have considerable therapeutic value. Border Terriers and their owners regularly visit homes for the aged, hospitals and prisons. Their presence gives enjoyment, revives pleasant memories and does much to stimulate interest and conversation.

Border Terriers have also been trained to assist profoundly deaf people by drawing their attention to telephone and door bells, and fire and other alarms. They have also been trained to assist people with restricted mobility by carrying out simple fetch and carry chores.

PAT Dogs
by Janet Thomson

Tiggy and Annie are both registered PAT dogs. For several years I have been making fortnightly visits to a local old people's home for tea and cakes. Annie is only too happy to sit on a lap and be cuddled by a frail elderly person; although Tiggy will rush around, tail wagging, waiting for her cake, and generally providing much entertainment for the elderly residents. Recently we have begun to visit a home for the mentally handicapped whose residents seem to love seeing Annie.

I am sure that all this will make our dogs sound like saints rather than typical Borders, but in fact nothing could be further from the truth. From an early age they have both chased (and caught and despatched) rabbits on most of our local walks; and muddy puddles, streams and, of course, the sea are an irresistible temptation to the pair of them – they are excellent swimmers. Birds, cats, whatever, if it moves, they chase it; yet they live happily with our almost seventeen-year-old totally deaf cat, happily sharing a chair or a basket, Tiggy in particular always cleaning the cat's face after she has eaten a meal.

PAT Dogs – Pat dog Bonnie and Nancy Anderton at West Cheshire Hospital.

Terrier Racing
by Tom Stanley

In the early days of terrier racing Border Terriers were not always welcome, but now that Jack Russells have again grown legs of a reasonable length, competition is much more even and much more fun. The sport, if sport is the right appellation for such a gloriously chaotic pastime, has no governing body, few rules and little which could be regarded as standard.   ·

Racing tends to take place at hunt and working terrier shows, though other events with rural connections have also realized that a session of terrier racing is a sure way to create excitement and interest.

Courses tend to be short and straight, usually flat, though a few of the more adventurous shows also offer a hurdle course. Five or six terriers are simultaneously released from traps at the start and then pursue a lure, usually a fox's brush, between crowds of cheering spectators, to the finish, where there tends to be a certain amount of discussion among competitors as to who should rightfully possess the trophy.

What is needed is a keen terrier, agile and fit, who will not be distracted by other like-minded terriers or by noisy spectators, and who is prepared to chase the lure. A few sessions at home are usually more than enough to teach a Border Terrier that a fox's brush is an object to be pursued at utmost speed.

Terrier racing is as much a test of temperament as it is of fitness and speed. Fighting terriers tend to be unceremoniously disengaged.

Inevitably what began life as a fun way of drawing a show to a close, or of passing a relaxed evening in hunt kennels, is nowadays sometimes taken very seriously, especially perhaps by those who sharpen up the competition by means of wagers on their dog's speed; though for the most part terrier racing remains a source of fun for any keen and fit Border and its owner.

Collecting

Interest in Border Terriers inevitably leads proud owners into collecting material which, in some way, refers to the breed. Books, including of course breed club yearbooks, magazine articles, pictures, cigarette cards, postcards, statuettes – anything which has Border connections is grist to the collector's mill and provides an additional source of interest.

9

Ailments and Accidents

No species of animal, wild or domestic, and most certainly including our own species, is totally free from inherited and acquired disease, or from the deleterious effects of wear and tear or of advancing years. Even so, well cared for Border Terriers appear to experience few health problems, and such problems as *are* encountered usually offer little threat to their well-being. It could be said that if major health problems do develop it is because Border Terriers are so seldom ill that owners are lulled into complacency. The breed's incredible stoicism may also obscure illness or prevent owners from realizing its true nature.

So Border Terriers are not one of the breeds which enable veterinarians to grow rich. They can usually be expected to live long and healthy lives and to reproduce their kind without difficulty. However, that should not be taken as meaning that Border Terriers are never ill or are strangers to accidents. In order to enjoy good health they must be born healthy, be well reared and well cared for throughout their lives, and enjoy a modicum of good fortune. Dogs which are born to unhealthy parents, which are not well reared as puppies and which, as adults, are not properly fed, housed and exercised, are far more likely to need the services of a vet than are those which are well cared for from the moment they are born.

Unfortunately, however, infections and accidents cannot be totally eliminated even in the best regulated households; advancing age, too, inevitably brings its own problems.

Illness

The signs of illness may initially be subtle, perhaps no more than an imperceptible change to customary behaviour: quietness, a reluctance to take exercise or play, reluctance to move or a tendency to adopt unnatural positions, all suggest to observant owners that something is amiss. Unusual coat loss, and a rapid increase in or loss of weight might also be indicative of a health problem.

A slight narrowing of the eyes, an elevated head carriage and tucked up loins all indicate pain; above all, loss of appetite should give rise to concern until an explanation has been identified. Sometimes we flippantly suggest that loss of appetite is most likely to indicate that the dog is either in love or dead – but in fact, once the effects of hot weather, advancing pregnancy, overfeeding, an unsuitable diet and old age have been eliminated as probable causes, the possibility that loss of appetite is a symptom of a potentially serious health problem should not be ignored.

Delay in establishing an informed diagnosis and instigating effective treatment may turn a minor problem into a major one.

This is not the place to catalogue all the diseases from which dogs may suffer, the majority of which call for veterinary treatment and not the fumbling efforts of inexperienced, if well intentioned owners. We will deal here with just some of the problems which may be encountered, and for which owners may need to provide emergency treatment.

Over-feeding

Border Terriers have healthy, not to say insatiable appetites, and are thus inclined to obesity in the hands of owners who over-feed them. Obesity will restrict their ability to move, play, even to breathe; it will lead to ill-health and will certainly shorten their lives. Over-feeding a Border Terrier is therefore a form of cruelty.

Swallowing Foreign Objects

Greed, allied with strong jaws and an inquisitive, playful nature inclines Borders to chew all manner of things. Plastic or rubber toys, hide chews, poultry and other small bones, any cooked bone and other unsuitable objects may quickly be reduced to small fragments and swallowed, with potentially disastrous results.

Prevention is obviously preferable to cure, but if a Border does swallow something which causes it to choke, upending the patient and unceremoniously striking its back may dislodge the object. Failure to do so calls for immediate emergency veterinary treatment.

Toys are important.

Fights

Border Terriers are not generally a quarrelsome breed. Their traditional occupation requires a sociable disposition but one which is allied to courage and tenacity when faced by an aggressive adversary. However, this very same occupation requires that they be effective and determined when involved in an altercation.

All manner of weird and wonderful, occasionally dangerous and often ineffective methods of separating fighting dogs are to be found in canine literature. The use of snuff, lighted cigars and even the insertion of a forefinger into the anus have all been recommended. Simple methods are most likely to be effective.

Killing a plant pot.

Avoid increasing the excitement by striking the combatants or by shouting and screaming. Unless you don't mind being bitten, don't attempt to open the dogs' jaws, and never try to pull dogs apart because that will only make any injuries which may be inflicted far worse than they might otherwise have been. Permission to panic is refused! If a peremptory order does not do the trick remember that dogs need to breathe in order to fight. Immersion in water, if suitable resources are to hand, is perhaps the easiest method. Failing that constriction of the neck, using collars as tourniquets or by hand, will quickly have the desired effect. For those of a nervous disposition, hanging the combatants on either side of a barrier – a fence or something similar – will mean that neither can get sufficient leverage to do great harm and when they try to get a better grip they will fall to the ground.

Once dogs have been separated, it is essential to keep them apart at least until tempers have cooled. Check both for injuries, and thoroughly cleanse and treat any minor abrasions with a suitable antiseptic. Keep an eye on the healing process, particularly of puncture wounds which may be deep and are inclined to harbour infection. Bad tears may need to be stitched, and injuries to eyes will also need veterinary attention.

Pesticides

The misuse of pesticides and fertilizers by municipal authorities, by farmers, by gardeners and even by dog owners themselves is a growing source of danger to dogs. The 1994 report of the Government's Advisory Committee on Pesticides (ACP) identified only twelve incidents in which poisoning had occurred following the approved use of pesticides. However, 211 cases out of 444 in which pesticides had been positively implicated arose from their misuse. In 115 cases pesticides had been deliberately used to cause harm.

The safest course is to avoid contact with all pesticides and the land on which they are used. The domestic use of pesticides should be strictly confined to those which are known to be safe, and even then used with ultra-cautious care. Dog owners should read the packets very carefully before they buy any product which is to be sprayed on plants or spread over the garden.

Stings and Bites

Wasps, bees, horseflies and other stinging or biting insects can inflict painful wounds on dogs. If these are in the mouth or on the neck the resultant swelling may impede breathing and require immediate veterinary attention. If they are in a place which the dog can reach, scratching and biting to relieve the irritation may turn a minor problem into a major one.

Remove bee stings by scraping them out, which avoids injecting more venom into the wound. Treat either with a preparatory ointment intended for insect bites or with more homely remedies such as a baking powder paste, calamine lotion or ice packs. An Elizabethan collar offers an easy means to prevent self-mutilation.

Snake bites in Britain means adders, and are extremely painful; and it is to be hoped that owners have the good sense to keep their dogs and poisonous exotic pets well apart. The punctures should be opened with a sterile sharp blade and the wound thoroughly cleansed, taking care to remove the venom rather than push it deeper. The dog should then be given a specific antidote as quickly as possible.

Dogs will occasionally pick up toads and get a mouthful of evil-tasting and poisonous venom for their pains. Wash the mouth well and try to keep the dog quiet until the irritation begins to subside.

Poisons

The average household, its surrounding gardens and public parks and gardens become ever more dangerous places for dogs. The indiscriminate storage or use of potentially lethal poisons should be a matter of concern to all dog owners. Prevention is, of course, far better than cure.

Allergies

All species are liable to have allergic reactions to naturally occurring substances. Hay fever, an allergy to one or several types of pollen, is common. Allergic responses to the many and complex chemical substances we use in our homes are equally common. Dogs may show their allergic response in the form of asthma, conjunctivitis or by sneezing, but are more likely to reveal an allergic response by scratching, biting or rubbing the affected part. The skin may be red, wet and exude a discharge, and there may be local or generalized hair loss.

Emergency Treatment for Poisoning

POISON	SOURCE	SYMPTOMS	EMERGENCY TREATMENT
Strychnine	Vermin poisons	Tremors, intense pain, seizure	Induce vomiting, avoid noise, veterinary treatment imperative
Metaldehyde	Slug bait	Excitement, drooling, tremors	Induce vomiting, treatment imperative
Warfarin	Rodent poisons	Blood in saliva or motions, etc.	Induce vomiting, intra-muscular vitamin K
Ethylene Glycol	Anti-freeze	Vomiting, debility, incoordination	Induce vomiting, give coating material, veterinary treatment to prevent kidney damage
Petrol	Fuels drunk or inhaled	Vomiting, gasping, tremors, coma	Vegetable oil by mouth, artificial respiration
Garbage		Diarrhoea, sickness	Induce vomiting, antibiotics
Toads		Drooling, sickness	Wash mouth, induce vomiting

Allergies cannot easily be cured but they *can* be controlled, and by careful detective work their source can often be pinpointed and avoided in the future. Parasitic allergies tend to show themselves in the joints and along the back. Atopic allergies are most often seen on the face and feet. Food allergies are often associated with gastro-intestinal problems. Contact allergies tend to show themselves on the paws and stomach. In each case, careful detective work may identify the source of allergy so that contact can be avoided in the future.

Some Border Terriers are intolerant of lactose, a component of milk, which gives them diarrhoea: the simple solution is therefore to avoid feeding milk or milk products to Border Terriers.

Contraception

During the time she is in season, a bitch will be attractive to dogs and her own behaviour will undergo change. However, there are a number of methods of what, in broad terms, might be described as contraception:

157

Products are available which claim to mask or disguise a bitch's condition from possible suitors. However, none are truly contraceptive in that they do not prevent pregnancy if a bitch is mated; furthermore some may produce unwanted side effects, and none will deter an experienced dog because it will quickly learn to recognize the strong and repellent scent which most of these potions have, and treat it not as a deterrent but as an advertisement!

The most obvious, and certainly in our opinion the best contraceptive, is to keep the bitch away from fertile dogs. If the bitch is properly supervised and, when necessary, confined during her seasons, she will not be mated.

Seasons may be permanently controlled by the drastic step of having the bitch surgically neutered – though for a well cared for bitch this, in our view, is unnecessary – or they may be subjected to temporary control by the use of hormone pills or injections. Spaying, however – as the surgical neutering of the female is called – not only prevents the inconvenience of periodic seasons, it also means that the bitch is permanently infertile, will not develop pyometra, and may have a reduced tendency to produce mammary tumours. On the other hand she may develop urinary incontinence, vaginal dermatitis, her coat may become sparse and of poor quality and she may become more aggressive. It is significant that in America spayed bitches are said to have been 'altered'. The Kennel Club now allows spayed bitches, as well as neutered dogs, to be shown, but unless they retain the appearance and characteristics of fertile animals the exercise is not likely to be successful.

Hormone injections offer the opportunity to exercise control over the timing of seasons without affecting appearance or behaviour, and without foregoing the opportunity to breed in the future.

Pregnancy Termination

If an unplanned or otherwise unwanted mating takes place it is a simple matter, as soon as possible after the deed is done, to take the bitch to a veterinary surgeon who can provide non-surgical treatment which will terminate the pregnancy without risk or harm to the bitch.

Pseudo-Pregnancy

A false pregnancy exhibits all the symptoms of the real thing, even to the production of milk, a period of labour and a display of maternal behaviour; however, it is a perfectly natural, if inconvenient phenomenon, of genetic origin in that in the wild, the puppies born to the alpha female could then be reared by an inferior female whilst their mother resumed her leadership of the pack in the hunt. The condition is caused by activity of the *corpora lutea* which, if necessary, can be controlled by hormone tablets and sometimes by subjecting the bitch to a Spartan diet and increased exercise; together this may induce a return to the normal cycle.

Parasites

Alarmist accounts of the danger to children posed by roundworm (*Toxocara canis*) are commonplace. Most have little regard for the truth, or at best, tend to misuse outdated information. Dr D. M Bryden, Prof A.S. Kershaw and Dr W.E. Storey in their paper *Dogs, Cats and Foxes in the British Isles* (1995) reviewed six recent surveys involving 2,296 dogs and revealed a maximum positive incidence of 5.8 per cent in a kennel of police dogs, and a minimum incidence of 0.4 per cent in a group of show dogs. Similar surveys carried out on 1,002 foxes revealed a positive incidence which ranged from 66.7 per cent in Windsor Great Park, to 9.1 per cent in Edinburgh. These compared with the findings of rather older surveys on London cats which revealed an indicence of 11.5 per cent in 947 domestic cats, and 53.3 per cent in ninety-two feral cats.

A number of conclusions may be drawn from this evidence, and particular attention must be drawn to two. The regular use of anthelmics, as with the group of show dogs, can virtually eliminate *Toxocara*. Cats and foxes pose a greater threat than dogs and account for contamination in areas to which dogs do not have access. We are not aware of any surveys which target dogs which live with cats or which come into close contact with foxes, but it would be prudent if Border Terrier owners who also own a cat or who work their terriers to fox were particularly conscientious with regard to worming routines.

Although even more effective cocktails of drugs may be just over the horizon, by far the most effective wormer is based on fenbendazole. It is the only wormer licensed for use on pregnant bitches to reduce prenatal and lactogenic transfer of *Toxocara canis*. It can be given to unweaned puppies, and has been shown to eliminate *Toxocara canis*, as eggs, in the larval stages and as adult worms. It is also effective against the tapeworm species – *Ancylostoma sp.*, *Trichuris sp.* and *Taenia sp.* – and against lungworm – *Filaroides osleri*. The product can safely be given to pregnant bitches and to puppies as young as two weeks, and after a routine course of three treatments it allows breeders to be confident that they send worm-free puppies to their new homes.

Ticks (*Trichodectes canis*) can be troublesome and persistent, especially to dogs which are exercised over farmland or whose runs and kennels are infested. Existing licensed products are not totally effective even after repeated applications, but a recently introduced product based on fipronil offers promise of providing an effective, single application means of control.

Dehydration

Border Terriers usually have the good sense to seek shade when the temperature rises to uncomfortable levels, but old dogs, and blue and tans in particular, may be susceptible to even a mildly warm day, especially when being exercised or if confined in an inadequately ventilated kennel or, worse still, in a car. Anyone thoughtless enough to leave a dog in a car on a hot day, even for a few minutes, can expect prosecution for cruelty and absolutely no sympathy from caring dog owners.

Prevention is better than cure. Seek out a shaded place and place a damp towel or reflective survival blanket draped over the a dog's back or over the cage in which it is confined; this will help to keep it comfortably cool even on a hot day.

A dog confined in a car, even one which is well ventilated, can on a warm day have its temperature raised to dangerous levels in a matter of no more than just a few minutes. In a short time the dog's temperature may rise to 104°F (40°C), when its breathing will beome laboured and noisy, the mucous membranes of its mouth suffused with blood, its saliva thick and glutinous and it may vomit. Action must be taken immediately: dip the dog in cold water, spray it with a hose or apply ice-packs in order to bring the temperature down.

Once the temperature has rise beyond 106°F (41°C) the dog's life is in danger. It will be unsteady on its feet, it may produce blood-infused diarrhoea and be in a state of collapse. An ice enema will help bring the temperature down, but at this stage the dog is very close to death.

Hypothermia

Dogs which are trapped underground for prolonged periods may become hypothermic, their body temperature below that which is necessary to sustain life. Violent shivering, lethargy and apathy, followed by collapse, coma and death are seen. If the dog is unconscious it should be revived as quickly as possible by rubbing it vigorously with a rough towel, wrapping it in a warm coat or in a reflective survival blanket, and taking it to a place of greater comfort. The warmth of its owner's body will help. A lukewarm bath, lukewarm hot water bottles, the use of an electric blanket, even the discreet use of a hair dryer will help to restore its temperature to normal levels. Once the dog is fully conscious, a warm glucose drink will hasten recovery.

Swollen and reddened ears, toes and scrotum are suggestive of frostbite; they should be warmed gently and an antibiotic cream applied. The thawing-out process is very painful and the patient may resent attention.

Fear

It is unusual for Border Terriers to be in any way disturbed by loud noises, gunfire, fireworks and the like, and any sensible owner will take steps to ensure that dogs are not needlessly exposed to such noises. Anticipating the likelihood of unusual noise and ensuring that a mild veterinary tranquilizer is to hand will help dogs of an unusually nervous disposition.

Car and motion sickness is probably caused by fear, anxiety or excitement. Puppies should be acclimatized to travel as soon as possible, and the experience should be made as enjoyable as possible. Travelling in a familiar cage often helps. In the worst cases veterinary tranquilizers may be called for.

Old Age

Advancing age inevitably brings health problems for Border Terriers, just as it does for their owners. The breed is generally long lived: we have encountered a vigorous nineteen-year-old, and have owned several which enjoyed their sixteenth birthday. The exaggerations of size, conformation and possibly temperament which shorten the already too short canine lifespan are foreign to Border Terriers. Barring accidents, a well cared-for Border Terrier can be expected to enter its teens in vigorous health. Even so, owners must accustom themselves to facing the deaths of cherished companions. It might sound facile to suggest that the death of a dog may be as difficult to come to terms with as the death of a human friend, but in reality the loss of a dog which has provided constant companionship for several years may have a far greater effect on its owner's daily life than might the death of a seldom-seen friend. It is now realized that the loss of a dog may result in trauma for the owner. Vets, not before time, are being taught how to handle the trauma.

A vigorous nineteen-year-old.

Owners who care deeply for their dogs must accept the duty, heartbreaking though it may be, to relieve their dogs of suffering which has become intolerable and has reduced the quality of life below an acceptable level. Euthanasia is the last loving service which owners can provide for their companions. Dogs can cope with blindness. Deafness may be real or feigned, but either way seems to offer little inconvenience, and reduced mobility seems to be accepted without rancour – but at some stage the quality of life may deteriorate beyond what can be regarded as tolerable. The owners of aged dogs need to be vigilant for signs which indicate the presence of intractable pain. No dog should be expected to endure pain for which there is no hope of early relief. The decision to euthenase a dog is difficult and calls for courage, but it is one which sometimes must be made, and one in which owners have a right to expect support from any caring veterinarian.

10

Borders Overseas

Although the breed began to appear overseas during the early 1920s, it was not until after the Second World War that it was to make a substantial impact outside the United Kingdom. During the last few years, Border Terriers have left Britain to take up residence in Australia, Austria, Belgium, Canada, Colombia, Czechoslovakia, Denmark, Finland, France, Germany, Italy, Japan, Kenya, Netherlands, New Zealand, Norway, Poland, South Africa, Sweden, Switzerland, USA, and Zimbabwe. Long gone are the days when the breed was little appreciated beyond its native heath. Many of the breed's overseas supporters are members of one or more of the British breed clubs and derive enormous enjoyment from their excellent annual publications.

We are indebted to friends from overseas who contributed material for this chapter, some of which has previously appeared elsewhere and has been updated by us. So responsibility for any imperfections or inaccuracies that have thereby been introduced is entirely ours.

Holland, Germany and Switzerland
(by Erica Bons de Wever)

After Sweden, Holland is the European country where the Border Terrier is most popular. Numbers have been rising rapidly. The breed was first introduced into Holland at the end of the 1920s. The original imports were Sandyman of Kandahar, bred by Wattie Irving, Southboro' Stanzo and Lady Ruby. None was bred from and so after the Second World War there were no Border Terriers in Holland. The first Dutch Champion was Harm's Southboro Stanzo in 1933. The next, in 1958, was de Raad's Ch. Golden Imperialist.

In 1951, Mrs Langhour-Stein imported River Lad, bred by John Renton. Four more Border Terriers followed him. Matings between Glenluffin and Raisgill Flego, two of the imports, produced no less than thirty-two puppies. In 1957 Mrs de Raad imported Ch. Golden Imperialist, the first Border Terrier to become an International Champion. In 1968, Mr and Mrs Bons de Wever imported the bitch Deerstone Destina and two years later Wharfolm Wickersworld, the first blue and tan in Holland. From about 1970 the breed began to increase steadily, both in numbers and quality, and for several years there was no need to import dogs. This situation was helped because Ch. Deerstone Dugmore was in Germany and Deerstone Decisive in Belgium. During those years, the outstanding dog was Ch. Roughdune's Estate Agent, a son of Dugmore. He really put his mark on the breed: he was happy, quiet, never aggressive and wonderfully sound.

Miss Crucq's Half House kennel was started with a daughter of Wickersworld and she later bought Dandyhow Knight Errant and then Ch. Mansergh Pearl Diver. Both had a great influence on the breed in Holland. During this period, Mrs de Raad imported several dogs including Gawr Thistle, Llanishen Argosy and Am. Ch. Woodsmokes Douglas. They were followed by Ch. Brumberhill Blue Maestro.

In Germany, Miss Wiebke Steen has without doubt been the leading person in the breed for many years. She started with a Portholme bitch and then acquired Ch. Deerstone Dugmore; more recently she bought Bugs Billy, a dog with mainly Dandyhow blood. The breed has recently become more popular in Germany with a number of dogs having been imported from England.

In more recent times Jurgren Rosner's Cheeky Chums, founded in 1979 on a son of Int. Ch. Bombax Xavier and subsequently relying on Plushcourt affixed stock, has been one of the most successful kennels in Germany.

Since 1986, Jorn and Diana Tillner's Maletartus kennel has imported a number of British-bred adults and puppies, including Oxcroft Tricky, Ch. Oxcroft Rocker and VDH Ch. Oxcroft Trader, Ger. Ch. Akenside Freckle, and VDH Ch. Thoraldby Tiptoes.

Some people in Germany use Border Terriers for boar hunting: they are required to use their brains and keep the boar busy without coming within its reach until the man with the gun arrives. Both British - and Dutch - bred Border Terriers have been used with good results.

Surprisingly, the breed was not introduced into Switzerland until 1960, and it has since made relatively slow progress in spite of the sterling work carried out by enthusiasts such as Frau Feuz and her Red Hunters kennels, Marlis Huoni and her Collinetta kennel, Elsbeth

Clerc's Rannoch, a well-known Swiss Scottish Terrier affix, as well as Elsbeth and Eveline Zehner's Woodboomers. However, supported by other enthusiasts, they are now getting the breed noticed and appreciated.

New Zealand and Australia
(by Jim Graham)

In 1949, Pat Gilchrist imported the bitch, Tweedside Red Soda, bred in England by Mrs J.J. Scott and imported in whelp to Tweedside Red Silvo.

Rosemary Williamson began exhibiting in New Zealand in 1973 with an imported bitch, Farmway Swinging Chick. In 1974 Mr and Mrs Jim Graham brought in a dog, Wilderscot Guardsman, and a bitch, Farmway Swansdown, to establish their Otterhead kennels. They produced Ch. Otterhead of Southdean.

There has been a renaissance of Border Terriers in New Zealand and it is to be hoped that there will not be a repetition of what occurred after previous introductions when the life of the breed was solely dependent on short-lived enthusiasm from isolated breeders. A number of new exhibitors, some of them already famous in other breeds, have taken to the Border Terrier and so the situation augurs well for the future in New Zealand. The links established between New Zealand and Australia, by their exports and their success in that country, should do much to justify this confident expectation.

It is thought that Border Terriers first arrived in Australia in the 1930s. The first recorded Border Terrier was owned by a Mrs Russell of Victoria. Next, in the early 1960s, Mr George Sheanis of Sydney, New South Wales, imported a brace of Borders of the Solway prefix. Shortly after arriving the bitch died, but the dog, handled by John Ellsin, became the first Border Terrier to become a champion and to win a Group in Australia.

'The Border Terrier Club of New South Wales,' writes John Caldwell, 'the only club of the breed in Australia, started as an idea.' In May 1981, John Caldwell – who had been in the show and obedience worlds for nearly forty years – wrote a letter to all the exhibitors of Border Terriers at the Royal Show held in Melbourne in 1980 suggesting that a Border Terrier Club be formed. He received a few replies which gave the names of other prospective members. Since that time, membership has grown from the original core of nine founder members to almost a hundred, being represented in New Zealand and in the UK as well as Australia. The Club's first Parade was held at the Queensland Showgrounds in February 1983. At this show, which was judged by the late Mrs Francis Sefton (then editor of the *National Dog Newspaper* of Australia), Robert Bartram's Rhozzum Venture (Imp. UK) was judged Best Exhibit and Dick Emery's dog Austral. Ch. Foxjoy Berberis was runner-up. The New South Wales controlling body granted the club affiliation in 1985.

Sweden
(by Carl Gunnar Stafberg)

The story of Border Terriers in Sweden began in about 1935 when Mrs Anna Bergman bought Happy Thought and Saucey Queen from John Renton. Happy Thought became an international champion, and Saucey Queen, who began her show career when she was eleven years old became a Swedish champion. In the early 1940s Miss Julia Geiger bought Burrens Two Pence from Mrs Bergman. Next, Mr Leijonhufvud imported Tweedside Red Joker, Cramaden Twig, Raisgill Risky and Portholm Mab. The kennel produced three champions, Mellby Marvellous, Micki and Blissy.

Miss Brita Donner acquired Mellby Monkey in 1950. In 1957 she imported four dogs, Leatty Linkup and Leatty Golden Randy, followed by Jessica of Thargill and the blue and tan Todearth Blue Jacket. From Linkup and Randy came Int. Ch. Monkans Tico-Tico, a Best in Show winner when he was seven years old, and Champions Trapper and Viva.

Julia Geijer's Juniper kennel was founded in 1961 with a bitch, Monkans Mymlam, bred by Brita Donner. She subsequently imported a number of dogs from Britain, including Wharfholme Warrentop and Eng. Ch. Mansergh Rhosmerholm Amethyst, as well as the Dandyhow bitches Sweet Pickle and Sweet Polly. All these imports produced a number of international and Swedish champions.

The Bombax kennel, owned by Gunnar and Carl Gunnar Stafberg (father and son), also started in 1961 with a bitch puppy, Monkans Mikron, bought from Brita Donner. The first Bombax litter was born in 1963 from Ch. Leatty Panaga Tesse; she had been mated in England to Smokey Cinder and from the litter came Int. and Nord. Ch. Bombax Despot.

At the end of the 1960s the Stafbergs imported Daletyne Danny Boy and Felldyke Bonnie Hinnie. Danny Boy quickly got his international and Nordic titles and became the top Border Terrier stud-dog in Scandinavia by siring no less than twenty-one champions. Bonnie Hinnie was the grandam of Int. and Nord. Ch. Bombax Nickname, who was the foundation bitch of Mona Hedman's Tallarnas kennel.

At the beginning of the 1970s, the Stafbergs imported Eng. Ch. Foxhill Fulbert, who after attaining his international and Nordic titles went to Norway. A little later, the Strafbergs imported Clipstone Clover and then Eng. Ch. Clipstone Guardsman. Clover was mated to Int. Nord. Ch. Bombax Lurifax to produce the two champions Bombax Tallyho and Bombax Titbit; in her next litter to Danny Boy, she produced Bombax Xavier, who became an international and Nordic champion before going to England where, campaigned by Jean Jackson, he attained his English title.

Mona Hedman's very successful Tallarnas kennel started in 1972 with a bitch puppy, Bombax Nickname, who quickly became a Swedish and international champion and also the mother of twelve champions. Int. and Nord. Ch. Tallarnas Nej Da was retained while Int. and Nord. Ch. Tallarnas Nypon Flinga went to Inger Morgren's Trientalis kennel. Mona then imported Dandyhow Observer who produced Lycko Par, Lille Orkan, Nickodemus and Fantomen, all international and Nordic champions.

Bombax Josefine, one of seven champions produced by Ch. Bombax Xantippa, became a corner stone of the Kletters kennel in Finland. Another, Leonine, was the foundation bitch of Kristina Gunnardontter's Urax kennel. The kennel has since bred Ch. Urax Fjallar from Felldyke Fulbert and the Int. and Nord. Champions Urex Garm and Grima from Ch. Clipstone Guardsman.

Margaretha Carlsson's Quisin kennel began with Juniper Jerrantop and Klabbette. She then imported Dandyhow Sherry Brandy and Int. and Nord. Ch. Bannerdown Monarch. The best known of the Quisin Borders are the Int. and Nord. Champions Quisin Yipayk and Quisin Yempella.

Krister Giselsson's Brackenhill kennel has produced a number of show and working champions, many of whom are descendants of the import Int. and Nord. Ch. Swed. Nord. and working Ch. Llanishen Ivanhoe, and of Int. Nord. Ch. Fin. and Working Ch. Cheltorian Midnight, who sired twenty champions.

The Redrob kennel, owned by Margareta Grafstrom, started with a daughter of Bombax Xavier and Whispering Hekate called Int. and Nord. Ch. Redrob Viktoria. Int. and Nord. Ch. Bannerdown

Butterscotch was then imported and became the mother of five champions. One of the best known dogs from this kennel was Int. Nord. Ch. Redrob Titus, who was by Llanishen Ivanhoe out of Redrob Viktoria.

There are many other breeders in Sweden and throughout Scandinavia who maintain small kennels that regularly produce winners; unfortunately space does not allow all to be mentioned. Although the Swedish Border Terrier Club Show is not a Championship Show wins are very highly prized. The number of dogs entered is often far higher than at any other Scandinavian show. Many, as at any club show, are much loved companions who might never do well in the show ring; but sometimes outstanding dogs emerge from homes that have never before had a show dog. All the major kennels, 'too, are represented and all are trying to win. As often as possible the club invites judges from Britain and then competition is especially keen and a win very highly prized.

America
(by Robert and Ruth Ann Naun)

Although there is no record of exactly when the Border Terrier was first recognized by the American Kennel Club, we can assume that this important event took place prior to 1927, when the first Border Terrier was registered in the American Kennel Club Stud Book. In the years before 1930, nineteen Borders were exported to the United States. Only three were registered in the American Stud Book: Barney Boy, bred by Messrs Dodd and Carruthers and imported by Mr H.S. Cram; Nessy, bred by Miss B. Hardy, and Blacklyne Lady, bred by Mrs Armstong, both imported by Mr G.D. Thayer. The first British champion imported to the United States was Rustic Rattle, bred by Mrs J.A. Simpson, and brought to the United States by Percy Roberts. The 1930s saw few Border Terriers registered with the American Kennel Club. The decade did produce, however, the first American-bred Borders to be registered. They were from two litters bred by Mr C. Gordon Massey of Trappe, Maryland. The first litter was whelped in Aiken, North Carolina, on 1 April 1931, and the second on 28 July 1931. Mr C. Gordon Massey, their breeder, had a number of Borders and, while he did not exhibit his dogs very often, he would exhibit at his home show. At the Talbot County Kennel Club near Easton, Maryland, in 1935, he entered eleven Borders including a number of important ones, Knowe Roy, Baiter and Red Twister, all out of Ch. Todhunter bred by John Renton.

In 1937, Mr MacBain imported Pyxie L'Bladnoch in whelp to Ch. Foxlair. She became the first American champion and produced Diehard Sandy, the sire of Am. Ch. Diehard Dandy, and Am. Ch. Diehard Dandy's dam, Diehard Betta. From Betta came Borders which would have important places in the pedigrees of the Philabeg and Dalquest kennels of following decades.

The breed made some significant gains in the 1940s, owed in large part to the efforts of Dr Merritt Pope (Philabeg kennels). Dr Pope was the moving force in the promotion of the Border Terrier in the years 1941 to 1946. In December 1946, Captain John C. Nicholson wrote to Dr Pope suggesting that a Border Terrier club be formed. Captain Nicholson and his wife had emigrated to the United States at the end of World War II and had brought with them Swallowfield Say When and Dronfield Reckless. By mid-January 1947, William MacBain, of Diehard kennels, wrote to Dr Pope agreeing to the need for a club. Soon Emerson Latting, who owned Diehard Dandy (the second recorded American Border champion) joined the group. Captain Nicholson and Dr Pope met for the first time at the Westminster Kennel Club Show in New York City in February 1947. They decided that a descriptive Standard for the breed was required. Their goal was to develop a Standard acceptable to both Border breeders and the American Kennel Club. Using the British Standard as a guide, they would enlarge it, and hope to make it clearer for an American audience. Dr Pope was elected chairman of the Standard committee and Mrs Nicholson became its secretary and treasurer. The embryo of 'The American Border Terrier Club' was formed. Dr Pope and Mrs Nicholson undertook to canvass American and British breeders for their views regarding the proposed Standard. Countless suggestions and comments were tabled and a tentative Standard was presented at a meeting of the American Border Terrier Club on 28 August 1948, at Pittsfield, Massachusetts.

The American Border Terrier Club now had a written Standard, approved by the AKC on 14 March 1950, and ten members: Dr and Mrs Merritt N. Pope (Philabeg), William MacBain (Diehard), Emerson Latting (Balquhain), Mr and Mrs Charles Schindler, General Edgar E. Humer, Miss Gertrude B. Dunbar, and Misses Margery Harvey and Margory Van Der Veer (Dalquest), who had purchased a puppy from Dr Pope. Dr Pope was elected President and Miss Marjory Van der Veer was elected Secretary. She held the post until 1982 and, with Miss Harvey, owned or bred over forty-four champions before retiring from the ring in 1983. A number of dogs were imported by Dalquest: Am. Ch. Portholme Matilda arrived in 1953 and was soon followed by Am. Ch. Portholme Max Factor, the sire of ten champions. Two years later came Am. Ch. Portholme Mhor of Dalquest, who was Best Border at the first Border Speciality in 1959, and earned his Gold Register of Merit by siring thirteen champions.

The next and most famous Portholme Border to come to Dalquest was one that Miss Van Der Veer and Miss Harvey purchased, Eng. and Am. Ch. Portholme Macsleap of Dalquest. Having already sired three champions in England, he came to the United States at the age of four and a half and went on to sire ten more. In addition he won the 1965 Speciality, arriving in the US only two days beforehand, and finishing his American Championship in four shows within four months. Mhor sired the first Border Group winner Am. Ch. DG's Wattie Irving of Dalquest, as well as Mex. and Am. and Ch. Bandersnatch Brillig, CD, and Am. Ch. Rose Bud of Lothian, later to join the Town Hill kennels of Mr and Mrs Henry Mosle. Another very productive kennel, one which has never had a prefix but has produced a number of outstanding ROM (Register of Merit) winners, was Mrs Marion Dupont Scott's. Mrs Scott died in 1984, but the Borders of her kennels continue under the able direction of Damara Bolte. Mrs Scott, along with Carroll Bassett, had a number of champion Borders in the fifties and sixties. Her most outstanding ROM Borders were the famous duo, Am. Ch. Rob Roy Buckler and Am. Ch. Shuttle. They produced American Champions Nonstop, Delta, Scooter, Buckshot, Concorde, Express, Razzle, Dazzle, Ransom, Contrail, Supersaver, Standby and Piper Cub.

The third important kennel with marked influence during the period after the Second World War is the Shelburne kennel of the Webb family. Shelburne and the Webb family have been associated over the years with the Shelburne Hunt, founded in 1903 by J. Watson Webb. This earliest recognized private hunt in the USA remained active until 1953. The Shelburne prefix is continued to this day by Mrs Kate Seeman, a member of the Webb family. Upon joining the family, Kate quickly became fascinated by the versatility of these terriers, who were great with kids, sturdy, good house pets, and also readily adapted to the hunt, to retrieving, and to hunting woodchucks, or even lizards when something more appropriate was not available. The first Shelburne champion was Am. Ch. Shelburne Slipper; her Championship was finished with three five-point major wins. The second was Eng. and Am. Ch. Lucky Purchase, bought from Adam Forster. The list of imported Borders in this kennel over the years is remarkable in quality and extent, and includes: Am. Ch. Chalkcroft Blue Peter, Am. Ch. Golden Fancy, Eng. and Am. Ch. Dandyhow Bitter Shandy, Eng. and Am. Ch. Brieryhill Gertrude, Eng. and Am. Ch. Jonty Lad, Am. Ch. Covington Eagle, Am. Ch. Dandyhow Sarah, Am. Ch. Deerstone Tylview Dusty, Eng. and Am. Ch. Deerstone Debrett, Am. Ch. Deerstone Decorum, Eng. and Am. Ch. Dandyhow Shady Lady, Am. Ch. Monty of Essenhigh, Am. Ch. Redridge Ramona, Am. Ch. Elandmead Psalm, Eng. and Am. Ch. Workmore Waggoner, WC, Am. Ch. Redridge Russet, Br Am. Ch. Cannybuff Cloud, Am. Ch. Workmore Tristar, Am. Ch. Starcyl March On, Ch. Am. Ch. Thoraldby Free Guest, and Am. Ch. Thoraldby Tomahawk. The kennel has also bred a number of American champions.

The famous Eng. and Am. Ch. Workmore Waggoner, WC, from the veterans class, was Best of Breed in the first BTCA Speciality in which he participated, and in the subsequent four specialties as well. A Gold ROM winner, Workmore Waggoner has achieved the distinction of

171

Phyllis Mulcaster's Ch.
Portholme Max Factor.

having sired the most champion get of any dog in this country to date. Although not used a great deal by breeders outside of Shelburne until his later years, he has at the time of this writing produced twenty-three American champions. Waggoner was especially productive with ROM winner Am. Ch. Redbridge Russet, imported by Shelburne.

Another kennel well known for its outstanding imports is the Trails End kennel of Mrs Nancy Hughes. The three best known of these imports are Eng. and Am. Ch. Workmore Brackon, imported in 1972 and co-owned with Nancy Kloskowski; Eng. and Am. Ch. Final Honour, imported in 1973, co-owned with David Kline; and Ch. Duttonlea Autocrat of Dandyhow imported in 1982.

Final Honour's daughter, Gold ROM winner Am. Ch. Trails End Peaceful Bree, was the foundation bitch of Lothorien kennels and produced twelve champions. His son, gold ROM winner, Am. Ch. Little Fir Gremlin of Arid, owned by Kenneth Klothen and David Kline, produced eleven champions. Autocrat produced eighteen champions, five of which were from UK import, Ch. Dandyhow Forget-Me-Not.

David Kline bred three ROM winners in his Little Fir kennel, Little Fir Gremlin of Ariel, Am. Ch. Little Fir Kirksman who produced ten champions for Mrs Betsey Finley's midwestern Woodland kennels, and Am. Ch. Little Fir Autumngold, who produced four champions.

Mrs Finley's kennels have been the home of a number of ROM winners, including Gold ROM Am. Ch. Little Fir Kirksman with ten champions, bred by David Kline; Am. Ch. Edebrea Dusky Maiden bred by Miss M. Edgar and co-owned with Mary C. Pickford and Am. Ch. Dalquest Rebecca of Woodlawn, both with nine champions.

Carol Sowders' midwestern Ketka kennels relied exclusively on American-bred stock and produced several Gold ROM winners: Am.

Ch. Ketka Swashbuckler, who produced fifteen champions; and Am. Ch. Ketka Gopher Broke with nine champions. The star in the kennel crown, however, must be James Ham and Larry Saganski's Am. Ch. Ketka Qwik Charge of Dalfox, whose many successes in the Best in Show ring were augmented by his thirty champion offspring.

The USA eastern seaboard has been the historic stronghold of the Border Terrier in the United States. Camilla Moon's small Highdyke kennel was based on foundation bitch Clipstone Cider Rose, whose only litter included two ROM winners one of which became the foundation bitch of Kate Murphy's Cymri Hill kennels.

Margaret and Harvey Pough's Bandersnatch kennels have a long history and have produced the ROM-winning bitches Mex. and Am. Ch. Bandersnatch Brillig, CD; Bandersnatch Beamish, owned by Lonanne Hammett; and Ch. Bandersnatch Jubjub Bird, CDX, owned by Grizella Sqilagyi. Another small kennel, already well known for Sealyhams and Airedales when Borders were added to the kennel, is Barbara and Lesley Anthony's Seabrook kennels which has had strong success in both exhibition and breeding. Their champions included Am. Ch. Concorde, a Bronze-ROM winner, who was the first owner-handled, American-bred Border Terrier to win a Best in Show. Concorde's daughter, Am. Ch. Seabrook Galadiel, has also the distinction of having won a Best in Show. Lothlorien Border Terriers have been closely associated with the obedience ring and the working trials of the American Working Terrier Association. Lothlorien's foundation bitch, Am. Ch. Trails End Bree, UD, was acquired by Joan Frier-Murza from Nancy Hughes. Bree produced twelve champions, among which were Am. Ch. Lothlorien's Jollymuff Tickle, herself a Bronze-ROM winner, owned by Diane Jones. Tickle produced Am. Ch. Jollymuff Crisply Critter, another ROM winner, owned by Kendall Herr. Over half of Bree's offspring went on to attain obedience degrees with one, Am. Ch. Lothlorien Easy Strider, UDE, owned by Nancy Hiscock, going on to get his utility degree as did Bree herself.

The Oldstone kennels of Robert and Ruth Ann Naun began with the acquisition of a bitch puppy, Am. Ch. Borderseal Bessie, by Ch. Clipstone Guardsman out of Chuck Wuca, bred by John Renton. Another puppy, Am. Ch. Dandyhow Bertie Bassett was subsequently acquire in 1975. Bertie, a Bronze-ROM winner bred to Borderseal Bessie, produced the Gold-ROM winner Am. Ch. Oldstone Ragrug. With Clipstone Cider Rose he produced two ROM winners, Am. Ch. Highdyke Alpha and Highdyke Twiglet. Bred to Eng. and Am. Ch. Workmore Waggoner she produced two litters, a total of eight

173

Gilbert Walker's Ch.
Workmore Waggoner.

puppies, seven of which became champions. Am. Ch. Oldstone Ragrug produced twelve champions from six different bitches.

Pat Quinn's Foxley kennels was founded on imports from Alison Mountain's Avim kennel. These included Am. Can. and Bermudan Ch. Avim Dainty Girl, who has the distinction of being the first Border Terrier to win an American Working and Hunting Certificate. Another notable was Betsy Finley's Gold-ROM Am. Ch. Foxley Bright Forecast, who became the sire of over twenty champions. Phil and Sharon Freilich's Freilance kennel had a dream start provided by Am. Ch. Krispin Tailor Made, who won Best of Breed at the 1994 BTCA Speciality, was three times Best in Show All Breeds and had numerous group wins to his credit. The kennel also competes in obedience and earth-dog trials.

Kennels that have arrived on the scene more recently, but that have already made an important contribution to the breed in the United States, include Teri Beverly's Bever Lea kennels, founded in 1981. Utilizing American-bred stock, Teri has already produced almost forty champions as well as a number that have won their CG or earth dog titles.

In relation to the history of pure-bred dogs in the United States, the history of the Border Terrier is a brief one. Both the breed's beginnings and its recent growth demonstrate that a numerically small breed is completely dependent upon persevering breeders. The future of the Border Terrier in America lies directly in their hands. The Register of Merit Awards (ROM) has been emphasized here since these sires and dams have very literally shaped the Border Terrier in America. Continuing to breed Borders of proper type, temperament and quality, and with the subtle distinctiveness of the breed, represents our major undertaking of the future.

Appendix 1

Bibliography

Some of the following are out of print but are still readily available, others are out of print and difficult to find, yet others have become collectors' items which are neither easy to find nor cheap to acquire. Out of print books may be acquired from firms which specialize in canine antiquaries, those which remain in print from specialist booksellers.

Anderson, T. Scott, *Hound and Horn in Jedforest*, (T.S. Smail, Edinburgh).

Anderson, T. Scott, *Holloas from the Hills*, (T.S. Smail, Edinburgh).

Anderson, R.S., Ed., *Nutrition and Behaviour in Dogs and Cats*, (Pergamon Press, Oxford) 1982.

Barrett, BS, (Kinesilogy) MS (Anatomy & Cell Biology), Robert, *The Question of Cryptorchidism. Is it environmental, genetic or just chance?* (*Dogs All*, Canada), April 1994.

Border Bladet, (Swedish Border Terrier Club, Uppsala) published annually.

Border Bulletin, The, (New Zealand Border Terrier Club) annually since 1995.

Border Terrier Club Yearbooks and Newsletters, (Border Terrier Club, Carlisle) annually since 1967.

Border Terrier Champions, (Border Terrier Club, Carlisle) 1991.

Breed Booklet (Border Terrier Club of America, North Windham) annually since 1957.

Border Terrier feature, *Dogs Monthly* (*Dogs Monthly*, Ascot) September, 1994.

Border Terrier feature, *Dog World* (*Dog World*, Ashford) September 1995.

Border Terrier feature, *Kennel Gazette* (Kennel Club, London) May, 1994.

Border Terrier feature, *Our Dogs* (*Our Dogs*, Manchester) April 28, 1995.

Bradshaw, J.W.S. and others, report, 'A survey of the behavioural characteristics of pure-bred dogs in the United Kingdom' (*The Veterinary Record*, London) May 11, 1996.

'Breed of the Month', *New Zealand Kennel Gazette* (New Zealand Kennel Club, Porirua) 1991.

Cavill, David, *All About Mating, Whelping and Weaning* (Pelham Books, London) 1981.

East Anglian Border Terrier Club Newsletter, (East Anglian Border Terrier Club, Huntingdon) published annually.

Edney, Andrew, *Dog and Cat Nutrition* (Pergamon Press, Oxford) 1982.

Evans, Jim and White, Kay, *The Book of the Bitch* (Henston, High Wycombe) 1988.

Evans, Jim and White, Kay, *The Doglopedia* (Henston, High Wycombe) 1985.

Fiennes, Richard and Alice, *The Natural History of the Dog* (Weidenfeld and Nicolson, London) 1968.

Garnett-Orme, Hester, *Border Tales* (Southern Border Terrier Club, Skipton) 1967.

Garnett-Orme, Hester, *Border Terrier Champions and Challenge Certificate Winners with all names appearing in a four generation pedigree arranged alphabetically* (Hester Garnett-Orme, Reading) 1953.

Gillott, William M. *Border Terrier Records, 1920–1993* (W.M. Gillott, Melton Mowbray) 1993.

Graham, James *Making the Most of your Border Terrier* (James Graham, Kaukapaapa).

Graham, James *Visualisation of the Standard* (James Graham, Kaukapaapa).

Hobson, Jeremy *Working Terriers, Management and Training* (The Crowood Press, Marlborough) 1987.

Horn, Montagu H. *The Border Terrier* (J. Catherall, Hexham) 1936.

Horner, Tom *Take Them Round Please* (David and Charles, Newton Abbot).

Horner, Tom, *Terriers of the World* (Faber & Faber, London) 1984.

Jackson, Frank, *Dog Breeding* (Crowood, Marlborough) 1994.

Jackson, Frank, *Dictionary of Canine Terms* (Crowood, Marlborough) 1995.

Jackson, Frank, and Irving, W. Ronald, *The Border Terrier* (Foyles, London) 1969.

Jackson, Jean, *Border Terrier Club Workshop Papers* (Border Terrier Club, Carlisle) 1994.

Jackson, Jean and Frank, *All About the Border Terrier* (Pelham Books, London) 1989.

Johns, Rowland, *Our Friends the Lakeland and Border Terriers* (Methuen & Co, London) 1936.

Kennel Club Breed Records Supplement, The, (The Kennel Club, London) quarterly since 1920.

Kennel Club Stud Book, (The Kennel Club, London) annually since 1920.

Lazonby, Thomas, *Border Lines* (Shiach and Company, Carlisle) 1948.

Lucas, Sir Jocelyn, *Hunt and Working Terriers* (Chapman and Hall, London) 1931.

Midland Border Terrier Club Yearbook, (Midland Border Terrier Club) published annually.

Moore, Daphne, *The Book of the Foxhound* (J.A. Allen & Co., London) 1964.

Morris, Desmond, *Dogwatching* (Jonathan Cape, London) 1986.

Northern Border Terrier Club Yearbooks, (Northern Border Terrier Club, Edmondsley) published annually.

O'Farrell, Valerie, *Manual of Canine Behaviour* (British Small Animal Veterinary Association, Cheltenham) 1976.

Pedigree Petfoods, *Best Practice in Rehoming* (Pedigree Petfoods, Waltham-on-the-Wold) 1995.

Plummer, Brian, *The Working Terrier* (Boydell and Brewer, Woodbridge) 1978.

Robinson, Roy, *Genetics for Dog Breeders* (Pergamon Press, Oxford) 1982.

Roslin-Williams, Anne, *The Border Terrier* (Witherby, London) 1976.

Russell, Dan, *Working Terriers* (The Batchworth Press, London) 1948.

Sandys-Winsch, Godfrey, *Your Dog and the Law* (Shaw and Sons, London) 1978.

Sandys-Winsch, Godfrey, *The Dog Law Handbook* (Shaw and Sons, London) 1993.

Scottish Border Terrier Club Newsletter, (Scottish Border Terrier Club, Giffnock) published annually.

Serpell, James, *In the Company of Animals* (Basil Blackwell, Oxford) 1986.

Serpell, James, Ed., *The Domestic Dog: Its Evolution, Behaviour and Interactions with People* (Cambridge University Press, Cambridge) 1995.

Southern Border Terrier Club Yearbook, (Southern Border Terrier Club, Tewkesbury) published annually.

Sparrow, Geoffrey, *The Terrier's Vocation* (Combridges, Hove) 1949.

Sutton, Catherine, *Dog Shows and Show Dogs* (K. & R. Books, Horncastle) 1980.

Thorne, C. (ed.), *The Waltham Book of Cat and Dog Behaviour* (Pergamon Press, Oxford) 1992.

Turner, Trevor, *Veterinary Notes for Dog Owners* (Popular Dogs, London) 1990.

Walker, Joan Hustace, *Hot Diggedy Dog! Dog World* (Dog World, Peoria) October, 1995.

Willis, Dr. Malcolm, *Practical Genetics for Dog Breeders* (Witherby, London) 1992.

Appendix 2

On 10 December 1909 an article over the pseudonymous byline 'Juteopolis' appeared in *Our Dogs*. It was probably the first, though perhaps not the most accurate or best informed, article to discuss the breed in what might fairly be regarded as a comprehensive manner.

Just as 'Cottonopolis' was used to refer to Manchester, so towards the end of the nineteenth century, 'Juteopolis' referred to Dundee. It remains uncertain, but it seems very likely that the *nom-de-plume* hid the identity of Provost J.C. Dalgeish, who for many years was one of the breed's staunchest supporters.

How aptly does the Shakespeare quotation of 'There are more things in heaven and earth than are dreamt of in your philosophy' apply to the canine world. Yet we do not require to go back into the lore of generations past to prove that there are breeds of dogs being unearthed from obscurity and brought to the piercing light of public faultfinders year after year; and the possibilities are that we only now are in the embarking stages of this voyage of discovery. I sympathise with the antique, despised, and rejected in canine flesh, and like to give a slighted or lame dog a lift over a stile. Men sneered when the West Highland White Terrier took the floor. Whose face is the sneer on now? The contempt disappeared when it was seen that there was a mint of virgin gold behind the little white dog, and through this reason his place was assured. When the Shetland Sheep Dog's recognition was being fought for, the Toy was ridiculed as being the outcome of a vivid flash of abortive imagination – waste of energy. Today the 'Shelty' takes his stand on recognised equality, doubtless to the opposition's chagrin. Again do we see the Sealyham Terrier call for justice; and yet another – the Short haired Skye – said to be as old as Adam, but only appearing today from the place he has made his hermitage for generations.

Why should these old and pure – so far as recognised pureness in breeding true goes – races of dogs, from absolute neglect, run a positive risk of running to seed and becoming extinct as the dodo? And then when they do make their appearance on the scene they are heralded with ridicule. When a dog breeds continually true to his type, he is and ought to be regarded as a distinct variety. One point which will, I think, appeal to all who in some degree studied the earlier history of dogs is that crowds of them (the dogs not the students) are undoubtedly manufactured articles although it may have taken them (the dogs) generations to breed true to type.

But it is not of pedigrees nor of dog manufacture that I desire in this article to write. Nor is it on those breeds I have mentioned that I presently intend to use my pen. It is of a dog of ancient lineage, and, outwith the scenes of his life and labours, in great obscurity and isolation, and of whom the fancier who follows him not is of knowledge devoid. I refer to the dog known as the Border Terrier.

To the breeders of Scotland and England must be given the credit of producing at least three varieties of dogs known, at the time of writing, as of distinct breeds. These are the Border Terrier, the Dandie Dinmont Terrier, and the Bedlington Terrier, which I will without the slightest hestitation or fear of contradiction say are, singly or totally, the three gamest terriers the dog world has yet looked upon.

Of the latter two terriers much has been written, reliable descriptive, and standard articles published on them. They have been the themes from time to time during at least the last half-century of innumerable and bitter controversies. Specialist clubs have sprung in this and the other side of the Border to cater for them. They are known and recognised and provided with a separate classification at the Kennel Club Rule shows. Thus while the Dandie and the Bedlington have been before the public for years, and still going strong in popularity, yet the Border has remained stationary – never moved since these two bade him farewell.

It is therefore to try and do for the Border Terrier that which has been done for these other two breeds that this article has been put forth. One could imagine that the sporting, fox and badger hunting instincts of the gentlemen who inhabit the rugged pastoral country have been imparted to the dog they claim to have raised in Dumfries, Roxburgh, and Northumberland shires.

But why is it, then, that this dog has remained in comparative obscurity? It is from as laudable a reason as any section of country gentlemen and sporting men could possess. They are conservative to the highest degree in protecting and retaining that innate gameness this dog possesses. They will part with their other most cherished treasures, but to part with or lean to the decreasing of this Terrier's gameness – *Never!* They say, and perhaps with some degree of truth, that the show bench has taken from the other two terriers part of their working gameness, and thus they are frightened that the showbench and the patronage of the public and Kennel Club recognition may do the same to the Terrier they nurture, cherish and preserve. The dogs, of which typical photographs are here given, have been given by some authorities of the breed the nomenclature of 'The Terrier of the Hills', which is synonymous to his having lived, breathed, and moved exclusively upon the highest hills forming the south-east boundary of Scotland and northern England. In these districts classes are provided for the Border Terrier at the chief agricultural shows, but it is only now and then the owners will condescend to bring their dogs to these exhibitions. From this reason, and this reason alone, the public have not had the opportunity of initiating themselves into the inimitable game, pert, attractive, and fight-till-death little dog this is.

The general appearance and, to put it in a nutshell, I may say that the Border Terrier can be compared as near to an Irish Terrier *with its tail on* as the West Highland White Terrier may be brother to the darker variety. People may think this is a somewhat extravagant flight of the imagination, but men who know the dog will follow the analogy. To further describe for the sake of fanciers who have not been able to attend Border shows, or who are not of the hill-scaling fraternity, a more definite description of the Border Terrier is necessary.

The principal features to keep in view are: the dog should be about 15lb weight and the bitch about 13lb; shaped like a miniature Irish Terrier, with a coat ranging in colour from all shades of grey, grizzle, pepper, or mustard to deep red, but never black, white or black and white. The coat, which includes an under as well as an over coat, must be exceedingly dense, and hard as pinwire in texture. Jaw and teeth strong and punishing, although not so heavy and strong as those of the Dandie or even Fox Terrier, as it is not intended that the Border Terrier should kill, but simply oust, i.e. shift his quarry. His eye should be small and dark, with a determined piercing look. Ears small, and carried smartly, like a Fox Terrier: not prick nor semi-erect. Body short and well knit, plenty of bone substance for his size. He must not be leggy, which would defeat his object of creeping to ground, and he must not show too little daylight, else he could not follow his master (who usually rides on horseback) the matter of ten or even some fifteen miles and more in the early morning.

That they are popular on their heath is evidenced by the fact that at Kelso and other shows where classes are given the rings were often crowded with good specimens, as many as twenty-six up before the judge and their gameness in the ring is a treat to behold. Other breeds may sulk and refuse to show, but this Terrier is ever ready for any emergency in the way of a fight. He is a 'Micawber' – ever waiting for something in this line to turn up. At a show in the Borders one of these dogs was benched minus the half of his upper jaw – a trophy of war; yet his owner offered to back him against any other dog to go into hole and shift his fox. In their labours they have to encounter the lion's share of the rough and tumble of a fox at a Border hunt, be it peat, cairn, or moss hole.

Naturally, it is incidental to the obscurity of the breed that efficient judges and authorities are scarce, or, as a correspondent puts it, 'They may best be described in the language of the old Highland minister when he referred to the number of real Christains in his parish by saying they were like cherries on an apple tree – few and far between.'

I am strongly of the opinion that if a club were formed for the dog he would spring into the forefront of popularity with quickness – aye, even that of a spit from a Winchester rifle, and I do not think he will have to experience the same antagonistic jealousy through financial element – as the Shetland Sheepdog underwent.

There are several breeders of authority of this Terrier and I give excerpts of a letter written by Mr Jacob Robson, of Byrness, Otterburn, one of the strongest adherents of this Border dog. He writes:

'These Terriers have been kept in the Borders for a very long time now, but the name "Border Terrier" is of quite recent date, being given to them because they were bred and kept mostly in the English and Scottish Border districts. They have always been bred for their working qualities, and are used with the Border Foxhounds, and North Tyne Foxhounds chiefly; Reedwater, North Tyne, Coquet, Liddesdale, and the Scottish Borders are districts where they are principally bred. My father, when he lived at East Kielder, had some very class representatives of the breed – about the years 1840 to 1850. Also Mr Hedley, Bewshaugh; Mr Sisterton, Yarrowmoor; Mr Oliver of Spittlehaugh; Mr Elliott of Hindhope; Mr Robson, Newton; the Scotts and Ballantines of Liddesdale; Mr J. Dodd, Riccarton; Mr Charlton, Chirdon; and Mr James P. Paterson, Snabdough; were all noted men. At present good Terriers are bred by Mr T. Robbins, Bridgefoot; Anthony Dagg, Gowanburn; Thos. Hall, Lightpipe; John Hall, Larriston; Dogs, Riccarton and others.

'My father and the late Mr Dodd, Catcleugh, preferred this breed of Terrier to any other for bolting foxes. They vary in weight a great deal, although 15lb to 18lb is the best size, as, when bigger, they cannot follow their fox underground so well, and a little Terrier that is thoroughly game is always best. Flint, a mustard dog we had here nearly thirty years ago, was small, but the best bolter of foxes I ever saw. He was slow in entering to fox, but when he did begin was so thoroughly game and keen that he never failed to oust his fox. The favourite colour is red or mustard, although there are plenty of the variety pepper-mustard, and a few black and tan. Their coat or hair should be hard, wiry, and close, so as to enable them to withstand wet and cold. They should stand straight on their legs, and have a short back, not made like a Dandie Dinmont, long-backed and crooked. Their ears ought to hang like a Fox-terrier's, but this is not a *sine qua non*. A strong jaw is a good point; not nearly so long in the nose as a Dandie or Scottish Terrier. They may be either red or black nosed, but the red-nosed ones are often the keenest scented.

'I have been told that the Terriers owned by Ned Dunn, Whitlea, Reedwater, were more of the type of this Border Terrier than the Dandie Dinmont, and I rather think, from what my father told me, that the Dandie of fifty or more years ago resembled the Border Terrier in many respects – more so at any rate than now. My brother has a painting of a well-known North Tyne character 'Yeddie' Jackson, in his possession, painted in 1820 or 1830, with a Fox-hound and a Terrier with him, and the latter is the very type of Terrier we have still. Jackson went by the name of "Hunting King" in North Tyne and Liddesdale.'

Appendix 3

Survey on Breeding Results, 1977–78

Reproduced with the kind permission of Elaine Davey M.A., Vet. M.B., M.R.C.V.S.

Preliminary Results:

Data received for 46 Border Terrier Bitches which were mated during the period 1/4/77 to 31/3/78.

Average interval between seasons; 6.25 months. Range 4–10 months.

Number of services:

1 service	27 bitches
2 services	14 bitches
3 services	3 bitches
4 services	3 bitches
unknown no.	2 bitches

41 bitches had 1 litter during this period
3 bitches had 2 litters during this period
1 bitch did not conceive
1 bitch had an abnormal pregnancy terminated after six weeks.

Duration of pregnancies resulting in live pups:

Average 62.09 days
Range 56–70 days
218 puppies were born in the 47 litters.

The average litter contained 4.64 pups[1], with a range of 1 pup to 8 pups.

Three bitches produced eight-puppy litters. One produced all eight live, and they were successfully reared beyond three weeks of age, one produced seven live and reared them, and the third, whose pregnancy lasted only 56 days, and was delivered by Caesarian Section, had one survivor, which was successfully reared.

Caesarian Section: 6 bitches were delivered by this operation, indications for the operation being: 4 cases of uterine inertia, 1 malpresentation, 1 foetal oversize.

[1] This compares with an average litter size of 4.0, computed from Kennel Club 1987 and American Kennel Club 1989 Registration figures. Neither include puppies which failed to survive to be registered and may also exclude mismarked and sub-standard puppies.

This admittedly very limited evidence may suggest either that litter sizes have fallen during the last twelve years, or that an unusually large number of puppies (13 per cent) may succumb before being registered.

Appendix 4

Report of first Championship Show to include Border Terriers
Carlisle Show
September 30, 1920
Judge: Mr Simon Dodd

It was disappointing that there was not a larger entry the first time the Border has been shown at a ch. Show, although some very good specimens were forward. *Miss Bell Irving's TINKER*, by *North Tyne Gyp*, probably one of the most successful sires at the moment, which won the Dog Challenge Certificate, is a hard looking little red dog, a little weak in his coat but otherwise a typical Border. From his markings he evidently is a workman. *Mr Forster's Dan*, which won the novice class was also a little weak in coat but a working looking terrier. *Mr Wm Barton's Liddesdale Bess*, the winner of the Bitch Challenge Certificate is undoubtedly one of the best of the breed shown; she is a nice size with a splendid coat, but could have done with a little stronger head. *Mr T Hamilton Adam's Ivo Roisterer, Mr Barton's Red Gauntlet, & Mr Lawrence's Teri*, were all nice Terriers – the latter two rather too big.

Simon Dodd.

Appendix 5

The purpose of this table, which has been well received by the geneticists who have checked it, is to enable breeders to work out degrees of inbreeding within a four-generation pedigree without becoming involved in complex calculations. It works like this:

1 represents the parental generation, 2 grandparents, 3 great-grandparents and 4 great-great-grandparents. So since Grove Willie appears once as Foiler's paternal grandfather (2) and once as his maternal grandfather (2) Foiler is 12.5 per cent inbred to him. However, Grove Tartar appears twice as paternal great-grandsire (3 3), and twice as paternal great-great-grandsire (4 4), and the pattern is repeated on the maternal side. So through his sire, Foiler is inbred (3 3 4 4) and to his dam (3 3 4 4) which produces a coefficient of 28.1 per cent.

Position and Frequency of Progenitor within Pedigree

Male Side	1	2 3 4	2 3 / 2 4 4 / 3 3 4 4	2 4 / 3 3 4 / 3 4 4 4	2 / 3 3 / 3 4 4 / 4 4 4 4	3 4 / 4 4 4	3 / 4 4	4
Female Side								
1	–	43.8	37.5	31.3	25.0	18.8	12.6	6.2
2 3 4	43.8	38.3	32.8	27.3	21.9	16.4	10.9	5.5
2 3 / 2 4 4 / 3 3 4 4	37.5	32.8	28.1	23.4	18.8	14.1	9.4	4.7
2 4 / 3 3 4 / 3 4 4 4	31.2	27.3	23.4	19.5	15.6	11.7	7.8	3.9
2 / 3 3 / 3 4 4 / 4 4 4 4	25.0	21.9	18.8	15.6	12.5	9.4	6.3	3.1
3 4 / 4 4 4	18.8	16.4	14.1	11.7	9.4	7.0	4.7	2.3
3 / 4 4	12.5	10.9	9.4	7.8	6.2	4.7	3.1	1.6
4	6.3	5.5	4.7	3.9	3.1	2.3	1.6	0.8

Appendix 6

Breed Popularity

The following table attempts to quantify the inexorable rise in popularity of Border Terriers in Britain when compared with overall Kennel Club registration figures. The system negates the effect of procedural changes to the system but tends to underestimate the breed's popularity by ignoring the fact that, over the years, the number of recognized breeds has increased.

Year	Breed Regs	Total Regs	%
1913	1		
1914	14		
1915	2		
1916	11		
1917	-		
1918	-		
1919	13		
1920	111	16689	0.66
1921	202	23692	0.85
1922	208	30931	0.67
1923	203	40918	0.5
1924	235	48050	0.49
1925	262	55529	0.47
1926	237	58683	0.4
1927	187	59383	0.31
1928	174	56099	0.31
1929	182	53194	0.34
1930	207	48784	0.42
1931	178	43876	0.41
1932	196	45914	0.43

1933	231	50392	0.46
1934	232	53600	0.43
1935	253	58789	0.43
1936	260	56319	0.46
1937	290	56496	0.51
1938	365	56557	0.64
1939	267	39614	0.67
1940	69	13857	0.5
1941	52	12447	0.42
1942	103	20977	0.49
1943	114	35256	0.32
1944	260	53428	0.49
1945	376	72314	0.52
1946	571	110785	0.51
1947	650	120088	0.54
1948	674	105281	0.64
1949	815	106644	0.76
1950	659	100150	0.66
1951	718	92952	0.77
1952	659	78708	0.84
1953	718	79057	0.91
1954	644	82050	0.78
1955	643	90218	0.71
1956	746	100557	0.74
1957	849	103919	0.82
1958	805	115678	0.7
1959	802	126099	0.65
1960	907	133618	0.68
1961	866	142743	0.61
1962	810	145489	0.56
1963	911	141317	0.65
1964	871	140562	0.62
1965	827	142988	0.58
1966	799	133585	0.6
1967	788	146046	0.54
1968	803	157229	0.51
1969	918	169918	0.54
1970	953	175074	0.54
1971	902	161065	0.56
1972	1026	183722	0.56
1973	1029	183784	0.56

1974	1051	187780	0.56
1975	943	160278	0.59
1976	477	79571	0.60
1977	340	55048	0.62
1978	868	136974	0.63
1979	1196	200864	0.59
1980	1227	201620	0.61
1981	1152	172358	0.67
1982	1291	172520	0.75
1983	1330	184899	0.72
1984	1362	184043	0.74
1985	1502	198290	0.76
1986	1449	189416	0.76
1987	1534	181436	0.84
1988	1411	160550	0.88
1989	2510	283915	0.88
1990	2434	270769	0.90
1991	2249	252524	0.89
1992	2488	240157	1.03
1993	2474	235893	1.05
1994	2766	246707	1.12
1995	3038	264091	1.15
1996	3276	273341	1.20
1997	3338	267171	1.25
1998	3479	258746	1.34
1999	3829	240801	1.59
2000	4312	247299	1.74
2001	4484	220799	2.03
2002	5339	226318	2.36

Index